# handmade living

Willow Crossley

# handmade
# living

40 step-by-step projects for
crafting a beautiful home

CICO BOOKS
LONDON  NEW YORK

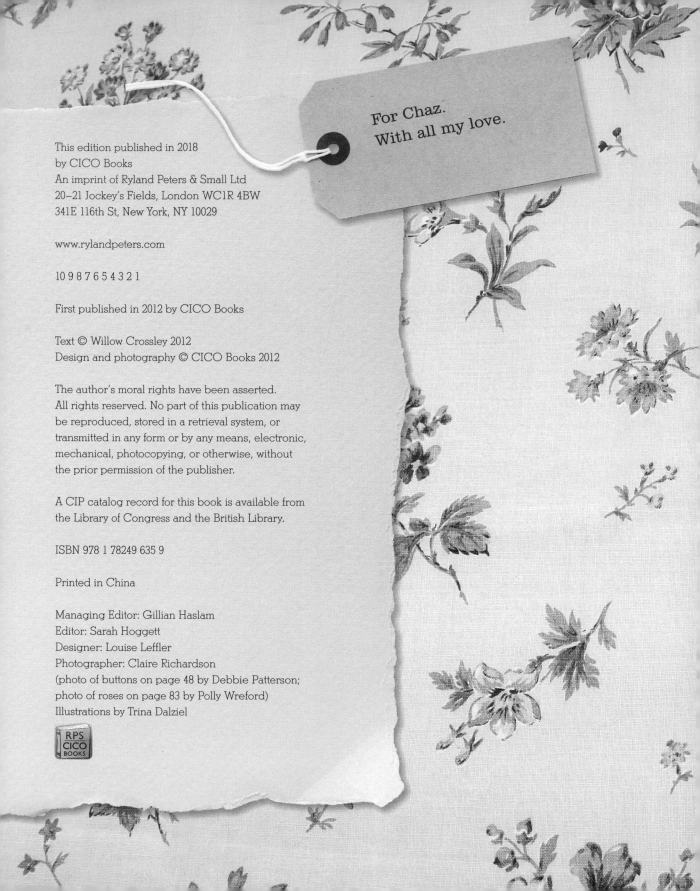

For Chaz.
With all my love.

This edition published in 2018
by CICO Books
An imprint of Ryland Peters & Small Ltd
20–21 Jockey's Fields, London WC1R 4BW
341E 116th St, New York, NY 10029

www.rylandpeters.com

10 9 8 7 6 5 4 3 2 1

First published in 2012 by CICO Books

ISBN 978 1 78249 635 9

Printed in China

Managing Editor: Gillian Haslam
Editor: Sarah Hoggett
Designer: Louise Leffler
Photographer: Claire Richardson
(photo of buttons on page 48 by Debbie Patterson;
photo of roses on page 83 by Polly Wreford)
Illustrations by Trina Dalziel

# contents

# introduction

Ten years ago I decided I'd worked in London for long enough and followed my boyfriend Chaz (now my husband) to the South of France. We lived on a vineyard and my new view was of Provençal hills and a permanently blue sky. There was so much space around us and so much room to breathe.

We had all the time in the world to potter and explore, but I am not good at being idle for long. I realized I needed something to do. The South of France has incredible brocantes (second-hand markets) and before long my firm Sunday fixture was to visit our local one, Jas de Roberts. On my first outing, I found a scrap of antique parrot print fabric that instantly made me want to get crafty. I felt this weird surge of excitement that usually appears only when I'm faced with a new pair of shoes, and I decided that this was how I was going to spend my time: crafting with beautiful, French, antique fabrics. And so in 2007, Willow Rose Boutique was born. I spent days rummaging around markets, vintage shops, and interior designers' offices hunting for scraps of fabric that I could transform into something beautiful.

For the first year, my repertoire was small. Apart from a few online orders from my website, most sales happened on the beach at St. Tropez. So, not surprisingly, I concentrated on what I hoped might be popular in this corner of a place that I admit couldn't ever be called the real world. Before long, the infamously chic Club 55 on Pampelonne beach became my main and favorite stockist. I can still remember the thrill of standing in the shop watching a customer buy up half my stock in one extravagant swoop. I was overwhelmed with excitement and stunned that people actually liked what I was making and scooted home to develop further creations.

Three years into our French adventure, we had our first baby—a divine little boy called Wolf, a.k.a. the Cub. Life in the middle of nowhere, a flight away from all our friends and family, suddenly got harder and we made the decision to give up our paradise and move back to the U.K.

Back in London I found there was less demand for such summery, beach-inspired products, so I turned my attention to indoor life (house and living-orientated products). Having never really immersed myself in home-making, I was astonished by a) how expensive everything was and b) how most things lacked any sort of personality.

So I began by simply adding details and twists to things
I already owned and went from there; I loved having things
that I knew I wouldn't see sitting in someone else's kitchen and
especially loved the fact that the transformations had cost so little.

I vividly remember at school despairing over my hopelessness
with a sewing machine—or any other machine, for that matter—so
from day one, I needed everything that I made for my boutique
to be easy and, as much as possible, technology free. I do now
own a sewing machine, but all it ever does is sew very quickly in
a straight line; no fancy business. Bar one or two of the ideas, this
is the ethos I've followed in creating all the projects for this book;
you don't need to be technical whiz or expert stitcher to be able
to make any of them.

I try to make my creations using only natural and vintage, or
"pre-loved" materials. Nothing is shiny, plastic, or glittery. I love
to create things that people want to give to their friends and to
have in their homes. I don't really make things that anyone might

need, just things that enhance your life (or at least the way it looks). I want to prove that it is possible to create beautiful things without being a genius on the sewing machine.

Many of the fabrics and tools that I use are found on eBay. A huge part of the enjoyment of it all is the actual search for the materials: the old grain sacks from Germany and the vintage feathers, ribbons, buttons, and feathers from Paris. Many more are free: much of the inspiration and many of the ingredients come from wandering around the garden or on country walks.

I'm always on the lookout for branches laden with fir cones to adorn a pretty table setting, flowers to press, and seed heads or rose hips for garlands. My ideas rarely need lavish quantities of fabric or equipment. Something magical can be rustled up from the humblest scraps. I'm a self-confessed magpie and find it impossible to throw anything away. I hope the projects in this book will inspire you to branch out and rummage. See what you can find and start creating your own beautiful home.

# Chapter 1

# to decorate

If I didn't live in a house full of boys, there would be flowers, frills, and fairies on every surface—but as the carpets are permanently cluttered with cars and diggers, I have had to compromise.

This chapter is full of projects that have a "use," but their main purpose in life is simply to look gorgeous.

# treasure domes

In the last year, I've developed a full-blown obsession with glass cloches and bell jars. I don't know why or where it began, but I can't seem to walk out of a shop empty handed when I find one. I have to say that my collection is getting quite impressive. I use them as mini galleries—a way to display my favorite, beautiful things safely and keep them away from the Cub's sticky little fingers at the same time.

RING THE CHANGES
I have nature-themed domes that I change every season. Think spray-painted holly come winter and dried poppy heads for fall.

My obsession with the cloches goes hand in hand with my love of old cotton spools, buttons, and threads. These make the most beautiful still life arrangements, and my bathroom would feel incomplete without the huge domes housing all the shells and coral that we've collected over the years.

The joy of these mini galleries is that you can change their contents as often as you like to reflect your own mood, interests, or the occasion.

At Christmas you could fill them with spray-painted fir cones, holly and ivy, vintage baubles, huge piles of clementines, or chocolate money. Bell jars also make wonderful vases and look incredible filled with sprays of mistletoe or painted twigs looped in. You could even hang baubles on the twigs inside and stand the bell jar on a table surrounded by candles, so that the glass sparkles in a festive way.

- SMALL WIRED FLOWERS
- THIN SILK RIBBONS
- PVA GLUE
- SMALL PAINTBRUSH TO
  APPLY THE GLUE

# napkin rings

I'd never even thought about making a napkin ring before I was asked to devise some ideas for Interiors Queen, Nina Campbell. She wanted to expand her range and asked me to come up with several designs that her company might manufacture. It turned out that my ideas were too extravagant to mass produce, but I had an amazing time creating them all.

**WHAT KIND OF RIBBON?**
Standard satin ribbon is inexpensive and generally wider than silk ribbon, so you'll need less of it. Very fine silk ribbon is more expensive, but I think it looks so much more beautiful.

## Posy napkin rings

These are mini versions of the headdresses I made for fifteen little bridesmaids at a friend's wedding, using wired flowers, tiny wooden bumblebees, and ribbons. Having had all that practice, I simply downsized them to work as napkin rings.

Millinery flowers are perfect for the job, as they are usually already wired. It's lovely to have a mixture of flowers: think about combining silk, velvet, and beaded flowers, as well as leaves. Even little insects or birds on thin wires would work. It's up to you whether to put decoration just on the top half of the napkin ring, which is all that your guests will see, or all the way around.

Here, the napkin ring is formed from the wire stems of the flowers; they are hidden by ribbon in the last step.

1. Choose the flower you want to start with: using one with a long wire will make life easier. Curve the wire around into a small circle, then attach another wired flower next to the first one by wrapping its wire once or twice around the stem of the first flower. Continue until you have the size of circle you need for your napkin ring.

2. When you've made the circle shape, keep adding flowers, leaves, and other decorations wherever you want them by wrapping the wire around the main "stem" to hold everything securely together.

3. Leaving a tail at least 2 in. (5 cm) long, tie a knot in the ribbon underneath one of the flowers, so that it's hidden from view, then wrap the long end of the ribbon around the wire ring, covering up the loose ends and bobbles of wire. I've never managed to get them perfectly smooth, but try to cover up the wires so that all you can see is the ribbon. Use a dab of PVA glue here and there to keep the ribbon in place.

4. Finish by tying the ribbon in a small bow or knot on the underside of the napkin ring, using the tail of ribbon left in step 3. Cut off any excess ribbon.

## INGREDIENTS

- NAPKIN RINGS
- THICK WHITE STRING
- PVA GLUE
- SMALL PAINTBRUSH TO APPLY THE GLUE
- SEASHORE-THEMED DECORATIONS: STARFISH, SEA URCHINS, SAND DOLLARS, SHELLS

**KEEPING IT NEAT!**
I find that it's easier and less fiddly to cut several lengths of string rather than one very, very long one —otherwise you'll just get into a big tangle.

# Nautical napkin rings

I've always loved those interiors shoots of elegant clapboard Hamptons beach houses, where the lunch table is beautifully laid with billowing white linen and drifts of sea urchins and shells meander nonchalantly around the wine glasses. I wanted to create napkin rings that would fit perfectly into that setting. The beach is one of my favorite places, so ordering a huge bag of sea urchins, starfish, and shells as my ingredients was an obvious first step for this project.

It was a struggle to find a plain napkin ring that I could transform, but eventually I found some smooth rings made of wood. You can use any napkin ring as a base, but having a flat side makes it easier to attach the decoration.

1) Starting on the inside of the ring, wrap the string very tightly and neatly around the napkin ring, applying a small dab of PVA glue at the start and end of each length of string. Each time you run out of string, cut a new length at an angle and then glue it down as flatly as you can, starting exactly where you left off. Keep going until the entire napkin ring is covered.

2) Glue your chosen decoration onto the top of the string, centering it on the width of the napkin ring.

3) Leave the napkin rings until the glue is completely dry.

# fridge magnets

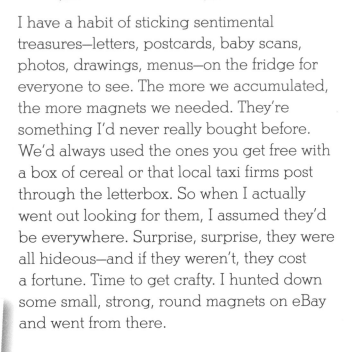

I have a habit of sticking sentimental treasures—letters, postcards, baby scans, photos, drawings, menus—on the fridge for everyone to see. The more we accumulated, the more magnets we needed. They're something I'd never really bought before. We'd always used the ones you get free with a box of cereal or that local taxi firms post through the letterbox. So when I actually went out looking for them, I assumed they'd be everywhere. Surprise, surprise, they were all hideous—and if they weren't, they cost a fortune. Time to get crafty. I hunted down some small, strong, round magnets on eBay and went from there.

As long as it's not too heavy, you can turn pretty much anything you like into a magnet. Some of my favorite things include beautiful antique buttons, wisps of gorgeous fabrics, and feather butterflies. I've also used natural ingredients that I've picked up on walks in the woods or on the beach, such as shells and pine cones. Small photos, Scrabble letters, and alphabet tiles are great ways to add a really personal touch, and you can even use tiny toys, such as small wooden boats.

1. Apply a dab of glue to a magnet, stick your chosen decoration on top, and press it down firmly.

2. Leave for at least an hour, until the glue is completely dry.

INGREDIENTS

- MAGNET, ½ IN.
  (12 MM) IN
  DIAMETER
- SUPERGLUE
- DECORATION OF
  YOUR CHOICE

READY TO MILK

Dutt 4

LAMU

U₁

R₁

A₁

WILLOW ROSE BOUTIQUE
WWW.WILLOWROSEBOUTIQUE.COM
00 33 (0) 6 10 51 10 41
00 44 (0) 77 66 00 68 94

# twiggy advent calendar

I love Christmas. I love everything about it—especially the planning, which starts in early December. Bring on the twinkly lights, the snow, the tree, the presents to plan and wrap, the lists to write ... I begin writing my lists in November, lapping up catalogs as they flood in. Making this Advent calendar is yet another excuse to start getting excited about Christmas as early as possible.

Making this project is quite a labor of love—not because it's difficult, but just because there are so many little bits that need gluing and cutting, tying and sewing. However, once you've made it, you will have it for ever. Every Advent you can bring it out and fill the little pouches with some new treasure. I mostly fill them with chocolates, preferably ones tucked away safely in wrappers. The idea of buying 25 divine little toys is heavenly—but in reality, time always seems to run out.

If you are making the calendar for children, why not go down to your local toy store, where they often have a "pick-and-mix" section of really inexpensive items? Then you can fill the parcels with things like toy cars, little bracelets, finger puppets, and beads—and all without breaking the bank.

You will also need a set of numbers, from 1 to 25. I used vintage bingo counters, but they're not easy to get hold of. Mine came from eBay and involved some serious bidding wars. There are lots of alternatives: rub-on transfers, numbered block prints, or even just beautifully handwritten numbers would all look great.

## INGREDIENTS

- FABRIC FOR POUCHES (I USED VINTAGE CREAM LINEN)
- RIBBONS (I USED THREE DIFFERENT COLORS)
- VINTAGE BINGO COUNTERS
- LUGGAGE TAGS WITH TIES
- NEEDLE AND THREAD OR SEWING MACHINE
- TREATS TO FILL THE POUCHES WITH
- PVA GLUE
- TALL TWIGS
- A LARGE JUG, PITCHER, OR VASE TO HOLD THE TWIGS (BELL JARS ARE MY FAVORITE)

1. Cut 25 rectangles of fabric measuring about 3½ x 8½ in (9 x 22 cm). It really doesn't matter if they vary in size slightly: I'm never very good at uniformity and quite like having a mish-mash of sizes.

2. Fold each piece of fabric in half lengthwise, right sides together. Pin and then hand or machine stitch the two long sides together. I love the rough edges so I leave the tops of the pouches unsewn, but you can hem them if you prefer a neater look. Turn the pouches right side out.

$\widehat{4}$ Cut 25 pieces of ribbon, each about 8 in. (20 cm) long. Decide what you would like to fill the pouches with.

$\widehat{3}$ Glue the bingo counters (or whatever kind of number you are using) to the bottoms of the luggage tags.

$\widehat{5}$ Place a little treat in each pouch, then tie a length of ribbon around the top of the pouch. Slide the luggage tag string under the ribbon at the back of the pouch, so that the tag hangs below, and tie loosely.

$\widehat{6}$ Now you're good to go! Simply arrange the twigs in the vase and then tie the string of the tags to them in whatever way you wish. Happy Advent!

# seasonal wreaths

I love wreaths. My Mama is queen of wreaths and they always remind me of home. They've always been one of those things that I thought only fully fledged grown-ups could make, but they're not. There's nothing really taxing about them, other than finding a good supply of twigs (and not losing your secateurs).

## INGREDIENTS

- AT LEAST TEN 45–50-IN. (120–130-CM) LENGTHS OF ASH, BEECH, OR WILLOW TWIGS, STRIPPED OF THEIR SIDE BRANCHES
- SECATEURS/PRUNING SHEARS
- STRING, GREEN TWINE, OR RAFFIA CUT INTO 1-YD (1-M) LENGTHS
- SEASONAL FLOWERS AND LEAVES WITH STEMS AS LONG AS POSSIBLE
- OTHER DECORATIONS OF YOUR CHOICE
- FLORIST'S WIRE CUT INTO 6-IN. (15-CM) LENGTHS

Wreaths have Christmas connotations and florists and decoration departments start selling them in early November to encourage our festive spirit. Of course, I love nothing more than having one on my front door—but I also use wreaths for year-round decorations. The twig frames shown here last for ages—you just need to replace the flowers and leaves when they start to fade and change your look with the season. In France, we made autumnal wreaths using pliable off-cuts from the vines and either left them as plain circles or entwined wild eucalyptus into them.

Wreaths also make wonderful table decorations instead of a jug of flowers. A summery one could be made with roses and herbs, with candles planted in the center or nudged in between the twigs.

Of course, there is no need to keep to flowers, although dried hydrangeas are ravishing. Let your imagination run wild! Depending on the season, you can incorporate apples, grapes, pomegranates, oranges, chili peppers studded with cloves, pine cones, or bundles of cinnamon sticks. Other decorative items such as shells, feathers, baubles, and little birds can usually be incorporated with clever wiring—and if all else fails, there's always superglue!

1. Take four or five twigs firmly in one hand, as if they were a bunch of flowers. Wrap string or raffia around the base of the bunch several times and tie the string in a firm knot.

2. Add another bundle of twigs near the top of the first bunch, securing it in the same way, then bend the twigs around in a circle. (It can take a few attempts to get this right.)

3. Wrap string or raffia around the frame several times and tie in a firm knot to hold the twigs together securely. Do this in several places.

4. Thread in long-stemmed flowers and leaves, weaving the stems in and out of the twig frame.

5. To attach decorations such as shells (with holes drilled in them) and Christmas baubles, center the decoration on a short piece of florist's wire, twist both ends of the wire together two or three times just above the decoration, wrap the wire around the frame, and secure by twisting the ends together again.

6. To attach fruit such as apples or oranges, skewer the fruit with a short length of florist's wire, then wrap the wire ends around the frame, then twist them together to secure.

### FROSTED OVER

For a cool, wintry look, why not spray the twig circle with white paint before you start decorating it, so that it looks as if the twigs have a light covering of frost or snow?

# fabric christmas baubles

I come from a family that has maddeningly restrained Christmas traditions. As children, we got used to pretending nothing was imminent until about December 23rd, when we'd think about cutting the tree down and dressing it with decorations that were past their best—although we loved them all the same for their familiarity.

Since I got married and spent my first Christmas away from home, Chaz and I have started our own traditions and put the tree up at the very start of December. The house gets swathed in holly and ivy garlands; wreaths hang on doors, inside and out; fairy lights are festooned in every room; and the carol music is on repeat.

We started our decoration collection when we lived in France, where they have some of the most chic, desirable baubles I've ever seen. My obsession with vintage-looking, glass baubles was born there and I've never looked back. In fact, I've just bought some sensational ones—silvery glass acorns with a ruby red thread that are heading straight for a garland around the fireplace.

This year, to make things a little more Cub friendly, I wanted to avoid having too many glass ornaments, so I decided to make my own. They are really easy to make and can be customized with whatever fits in with your own Christmas look. I started off using a mish-mash of different-colored fabrics for each bauble, but decided in the end that I preferred it when each ball was made from only one pattern.

## FESTIVE FEATHERS

You can also use feathers instead of fabric. It's much more fiddly, but they look amazing when finished. I find it best to do them in two sessions, as otherwise they get too sticky and end up looking messy.

INGREDIENTS

- POLYSTYRENE BALLS
- PVA GLUE
- WATER
- SMALL PAINTBRUSH
- SCISSORS
- SCRAPS OF FABRIC
- DRESSMAKING PINS
- THREAD

(1) Cut the fabric into small pieces. The shape is not important.

(2) Mix equal amounts of PVA glue and water. Using a small paintbrush, brush the glue onto the bauble and start sticking on the bits of fabric, overlapping them slightly so that there are no gaps. Smooth the fabric down by painting the glue-and-water mix over the top of it.

3) If the fabric puckers or bubbles, simply snip into it with scissors, lift it up, and smooth it down again with your fingers.

4) Stick some dressmaker's pins all around the bauble in a straight line from top to bottom and back up to the top again.

5) Measure the circumference of the bauble plus how long you want the drop to be, and cut a piece of thread to twice this length. Fold the thread in half. Starting at the top of the bauble, pull out each pin in turn a little, wrap the cut ends of the thread around the pin, then push the pin back into the bauble to secure. Repeat around all the pins in the bauble until you get back up to the top again; the excess thread will be in a loop from which you can hang your fabric decoration.

**CHOOSING A THEME**
If you prefer a truly coordinated look, choose a limited color palette for the fabrics. Or for a full-on festive theme, use scraps of fabric printed with Christmas motifs.

# embroidered notecards

I have such a thing about stationery that it's almost an obsession. One of my few fond memories of new school terms was the prospect of visiting my local stationery store. I'd come home thrilled with my pristine file paper, new pencil case full of sharp pencils and felt-tipped pens, and the oh-so-smooth, creamy writing paper with matching envelopes. Nothing's changed and I still get butterflies when I see an array of notecards in tissue-lined envelopes.

As much as I adore expensive writing paper and cards, I am reluctant to pay a lot for something that will be ripped open and thrown in the bin straightaway. This is why I've started making my own. The ones that get the most attention are these embroidered ones. You can make them as simple or as intricate as you like—and if you have a swanky sewing machine that embroiders for you, you'll almost be able to make them with your eyes shut.

To begin with, I spent hours trawling the Internet looking for free machine embroidery patterns, which I then loosely copied down in pencil on the card I was using. As I got more practiced at the embroidery, I would take my needle and poke it through the card wherever took my fancy. Making a border is very simple, as you just have to sew in a straight line. Vary the look by using different stitches: blanket stitch is one of my favorites for stitching around the edges.

For me, simple is usually better. With these notecards, however, I find that layering plain card over pretty wallpaper (or vice versa) and color coordinating the embroidery makes them look a little more professional.

1. Using a craft knife and steel rule on a cutting mat, cut out the cardstock to the size and shape that you want. Alternatively, use a ready-made card blank (available from hobby and stationery stores).

2. If you want your notecard to open out, so that you can write your message on the inside, mark the center top and bottom faintly in pencil on the back. Place a metal rule in between the two marks and, using a craft knife, lightly score along the side of the rule, then fold along the scoreline.

3. Lightly trace your chosen design onto the front of the notecard, or draw it freehand.

GLAM IT UP
For party invitations, think about using variegated and sparkly metallic embroidery flosses (threads).

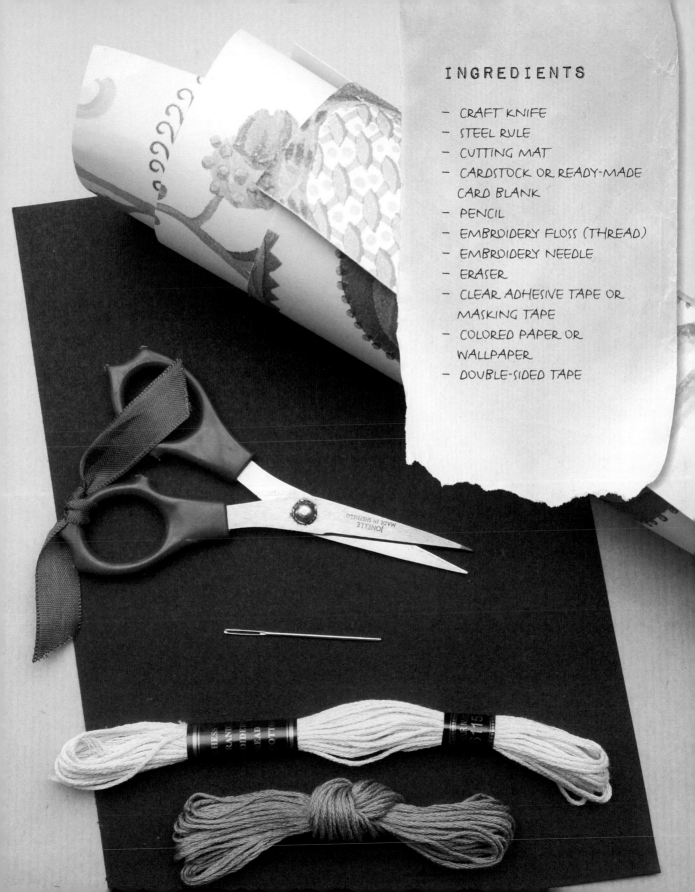

# INGREDIENTS

- CRAFT KNIFE
- STEEL RULE
- CUTTING MAT
- CARDSTOCK OR READY-MADE CARD BLANK
- PENCIL
- EMBROIDERY FLOSS (THREAD)
- EMBROIDERY NEEDLE
- ERASER
- CLEAR ADHESIVE TAPE OR MASKING TAPE
- COLORED PAPER OR WALLPAPER
- DOUBLE-SIDED TAPE

4 Put a layer of newspaper or a towel on your work surface to protect it. Using a sharp needle, pierce holes along your drawn lines to mark the start and end of each stitch. Alternatively, set your sewing machine to its longest stitch length and carefully sew over the lines. Remember, you're just piercing holes—so you won't need to thread the needle.

5 Thread your needle, knot the end of the thread, and bring the needle up through the first hole from the back of the card to the front. Take the needle down through the next hole to make the first stitch, then bring it up again at the point where you want the next stitch to start. Carefully erase any pencil marks.

6 To finish off each section of stitching, knot the embroidery floss (thread) on the back of the card or stick a small piece of adhesive or masking tape over the end to prevent it from unraveling.

7 Cut another piece of thin cardstock, colored paper, or patterned wallpaper the same size as the embroidered card. Using double-sided tape, stick it to the back of the embroidered card to hide the knots.

# to hang

In a dream world, every wall in our house would be covered with expensive art works —a Picasso here, a little Mary Newcomb there. In reality, of course, that's not an option, so for now we're making do with my handmade creations.

By framing some of your favorite things —whether it's a sentimental fragment of fabric, a print of a much-loved painting, or a ravishing collection of buttons—you can easily transform your walls into mini galleries of your own.

# initial art

These ideas for initial art make really good and unusual presents for children, perhaps for a christening.

All you have to do is draw an outline of the initial you want to make. If you want a perfect shape, you can always find initial letters on the Internet and then print them out for free. Google "outline of the initial "W", for example, and then choose the one you like, print it out, and you're ready to go.

I've tried quite a few colored paper backgrounds, but I keep coming back to plain old white, for some reason—although I do love using fabric, too.

You now need to choose what you're going to want to have as the "filling." Glitter, stamps, newspaper or magazine cuttings, and scraps of fabric all make great fillings—and you may be able to find stamps and patterned fabrics on a theme to suit the recipient. For 3-D impact, experiment with buttons, old coloring pencils and crayons, crystals, or shells. In fact, you can use more or less anything you want. I remember making pictures like these at school with pasta and rice when I was about six, although pasta probably wouldn't be top of my list these days!

If you're using something like pencils as the filling, it's best to use a fairly heavyweight cardstock, otherwise the weight of the filling will cause the piece to buckle.

1. Draw an outline of the initial you want to make on your chosen background material. If you've printed off an initial from the Internet or traced it from a book, cut out the shape and glue it as smoothly as possible to the background.

2. Using a small paintbrush, apply glue to the inside of the shape. You may find it easier to work on a small section at a time, rather than fill in the whole shape with glue at the outset.

3. Working quickly before the glue dries, starting from the outside and working inward, press your chosen filling onto the glue. It's important to get a neat, crisp outline, so take particular care around the edges.

4. Leave your initial art lying flat until the glue has completely dried, then place it in a frame, ready to hang.

## STICKY STUFF

Ordinary PVA glue works for most lightweight things, as does double-sided tape—but if your filling is a bit heavier (shells, pebbles, or metal washers, for example), superglue is a better option.

# stamp art

I'd never thought about making an artwork with stamps until one day, wandering around Welshpool market in mid Wales, I came across an old cardboard box full of the most exquisite old stamps nestled among muddy shovels and spades, spare tractor parts, and garden plants. They were all beautifully mounted on bits of cardboard and protected by special crinkly paper. I had absolutely no idea what I was going to do with them, but they were too mesmerizing to leave behind.

## INGREDIENTS

- PENCIL
- CARDSTOCK
- LOTS OF OLD STAMPS
- DOUBLE-SIDED TAPE
- SCISSORS
- FRAME

I began by taking a lot of arty photos of them and then decided that they would get far more appreciation if they were hanging on a wall in some way. The stamps are so bright and colorful that I immediately thought of making something aimed at children—something the Cub would like in his bedroom, perhaps.

Most of the stamps I've used here are actually ones I found on eBay. Amazon also has hundreds that you can buy in special themed packs, flowers and birds being my absolute favorites.

1 Using a pencil, draw a faint outline of the shape you're creating on a piece of cardstock. If you're not confident about your drawing skills, download a suitable copyright-free shape from the Internet, print it out, cut around the outline, and stick it onto your background card.

2) Work out where you're going to put the stamps before you stick them down.

3) Cut small pieces of double-sided tape and stick them down around the edges of the shape. When you're ready, remove the backing paper from the tape and start sticking the stamps down. Start from the outside and work your way in.

4) Fill in the middle of the shape in the same way, overlapping the stamps and placing them at different angles to add visual interest. If necessary, cut the stamps to size with scissors before you stick them down.

5) Place your artwork in a frame, ready to hang.

# memory box

I thought about pretending I'd made this myself, but honesty got the better of me. All the credit for this divine memory box goes to my Mama. She made it for the Cub when he was born and it's now one of my favorite things in the world. I'm sure I've said it before in this book, but I really feel that personal presents are always the best. They have that special edge over store-bought things, no matter how lavish they may be. It's the time, thought, and love that has been poured into them that makes homemade presents such treasures.

This box, being for the Cub, has been filled with a nostalgic boy-orientated collection of family mementos: old black-and-white framed photos, vintage toy cars, my father's favorite toy tractor, a wooden animal or two, a letter for him to read when he's older, rolled up like a scroll, and some miniature wooden battle ships. As a finishing touch, my Mama then découpaged the back of each compartment with stamps from my great-grandmother's collection.

You can make a memory box as a present or just for yourself. What goes inside is entirely up to you, as long as each compartment is filled with beautiful objects. If you want to have something other than stamps as a background, you could use vintage postcards, wallpaper samples, squares of fabric, or paint.

## INGREDIENTS

- A WOODEN, SHADOW BOX FRAME WITH COMPARTMENTS OR SHELVES
- PAINT IN A COLOR OF YOUR CHOICE (OPTIONAL)
- DECORATION FOR THE BACK WALL
- PVA GLUE
- SMALL PAINTBRUSH
- SPECIAL TREASURES TO PUT IN THE SPACES
- LOW-TACK PUTTY

1. If you don't like the color of your box frame, paint it in the color of your choice and leave to dry completely.

2. Then decorate the back wall of each compartment. Cut your chosen backgrounds to the right size and decide what you're going to use in each compartment. Using a paintbrush, apply PVA glue to each back wall in turn, then stick on the background. Leave to dry.

3. Arrange the treasures in the spaces. It's worth spending time trying out different arrangements, so that you get a good balance and plenty of variety.

4. Fix the treasures in place, using low-tack putty so that they can be taken out and admired.

## FIXING THE TREASURES

Low-tack putty holds the treasures in place. It's not a good idea to use it on precious letters or documents as, although it's designed to fix posters to walls, it can damage the fibers of paper.

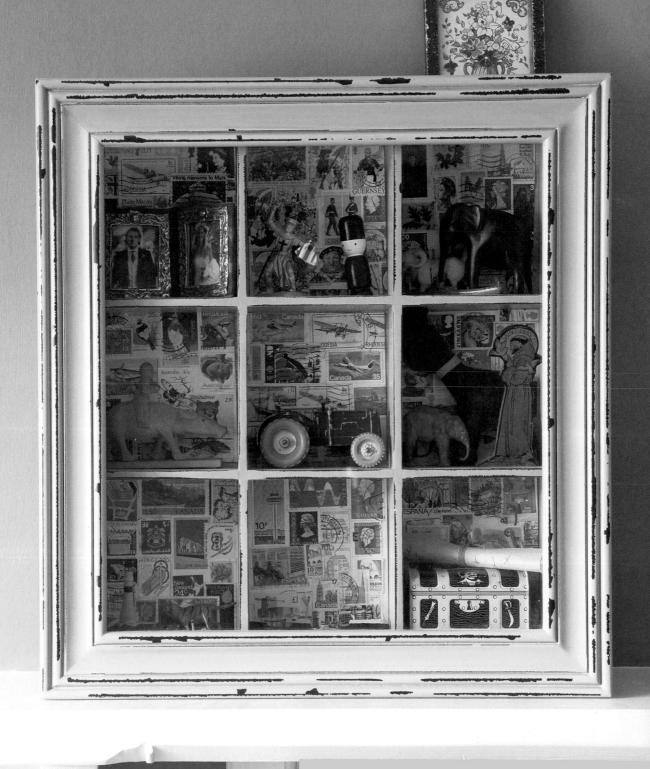

# printers' trays

I give all the credit for these to my brother Ned, who bought
his first printers' tray about eight years ago and has collected
them ever since. He now has a wall where six hang in a row,
crammed with quirky treasures. Every time I visit him I sit for
hours, mesmerized by them, checking out his latest additions.

My trays came from a flea market in France,
where there were huge stacks of them piled
up on top of each other. In a dream world,
I'd have a whole wall of them. (Not that I'm
in competition with Ned, of course.) But to
do a whole wall would need a lot of trinkets
and a lot of time.

My trays aren't really themed—they're just
full of bits and pieces that I've accumulated
over time. When I find a new treasure,
I just swap it with one of the things I'm
less attached to. Not surprisingly, shells
feature quite highly in mine and I am
planning a fully nautical one for our blue
bathroom. I'm going to fill it with shells,
starfish, driftwood, wisps of seaweed, cuttle
fish, phials of sand, small wooden boats—any
of the treasures we've found on one of our
many beachcombing trips.

If you feel like getting fiddly, you
could also découpage the back of each
compartment with old postage stamps to
make the background different (see page 54).

There's no need to tell you how to make
up the trays, as it's too simple for words.
All I suggest is that you put them up on the
wall before you start filling the compartments.
If you do it the other way round, the moment
you lift them up, the treasures all fall straight
to the floor.

## THEMES FOR PRINTERS' TRAYS

- TRAYS THEMED BY COLOR
- DRIED FLOWERS AND SEED HEADS (POPPY HEADS AND LOVE-IN-A-MIST LOOK DIVINE)
- FOSSILS
- DRIFTWOOD
- VINTAGE TOY CARS
- ANTIQUE COTTON REELS
- TOY SOLDIERS
- DOLL HOUSE FURNITURE

## WHERE TO BUY PRINTERS' TRAYS

Recently, I've been noticing more and
more printers' trays in little antique
and vintage shops and stalls; eBay, too,
is always a good place to source them.

# scrabble art

I've always wished that I was slightly better at Scrabble. Recently, I've been putting my low scores down to the fact that I've been borrowing letters to make these Scrabble arts. I love using the old wooden Scrabble letters to make these. Of course, you can use the more modern plastic ones, which are easier to find and not as expensive; I just prefer the look of the wooden ones.

## INGREDIENTS

- CARDSTOCK OR COLORED PAPER FOR BACKGROUND
- DOUBLE-SIDED TAPE
- SCRABBLE LETTERS
- FRAME

When I make these, I can easily spend hours just trying to work out sentences or phrases that I can arrange so the words interlock and look aesthetically good, too. I've often given up trying to make clever pieces and just make them with everyday sayings and phrases. Questions work well: a "Marry me?" for your intended, perhaps, or "Mr and Mrs So and So" for a wedding gift, or "The Old Farm House" for a housewarming present. Or how about a nursery rhyme for a young baby? I made "Twinkle, Twinkle, Little Star" for my godson Inigo, and put it on a background of starry wallpaper, which looks so sweet in his room.

1 First, decide what words or phrases you want to spell out and collect all the Scrabble letters together. There's nothing more annoying than starting to stick all the letters in place and then realizing some are missing.

2 Choose an appropriate background. Depending on your message and the person you're making it for, this might be a piece of patterned paper, a stenciled or printed shape such as a heart or star or a drawing with space left alongside for the letters. If the background paper is thin, stick it to a piece of thicker cardstock using double-sided tape.

3 Lay the Scrabble letters on the background. Move them around, trying out different angles and positions.

4 When you're happy with the arrangement, lift up each letter in turn, apply a small piece of double-sided tape to the back, and press it down onto the background. Place your finished artwork in a frame, ready to hang.

**SMOOTH AS SILK**
You can use glue to stick the tiles down but, if you have it, double-sided tape will ensure that the paper you're sticking it to will stay smooth and not bubble.

## INGREDIENTS

- AS MANY MAGAZINES AS YOU CAN GET HOLD OF
- SMALL SCISSORS
- SOFT PENCIL
- SCRAP PAPER
- WATERCOLOR PAPER OR CARDSTOCK FOR BACKGROUND
- FINE-NOSED PLIERS OR TWEEZERS
- PVA GLUE
- SMALL PAINTBRUSH
- KNEADED ERASER
- FRAME

# word art

When I was first given pocket money, I would spend the lot on magazines—there is something glossily indulgent about them that I never tire of. When I started making Word Arts, I had a proper excuse to buy them: they became justifiable expenses. And it really wasn't my fault that it's the most expensive magazines that use my favorite fonts and thicker paper...

The last four generations on my mother's side of the family have all been writers. I sometimes wonder if I subconsciously chose a degree in journalism because I hoped their talents might have filtered down to me. I've always thought being a writer was such a romantic profession: I envisage writing, looking out to sea from my white clapboard house, gauzy white curtains blowing in the breeze. I can't quite imagine when or how that might happen, but I can still live in hope.

As much as I love writing, however, page after page of black-and-white text can sometimes be a bit dull. Sadly, drawing is not my forte, so the idea of creating children's stories with divine illustrations was never going to happen.

My Word Arts are a happy combination of my love of words and my love of magazines. I write a story, often with a specific occasion or person in mind, then scour through my stacks of magazines to find the words I need. They are time consuming to make, but not at all difficult: all you need is patience and a steady hand. I love to use a heavyweight watercolor paper as the background, as it's just a little more substantial than everyday drawing paper. If you can't get hold of it, use the thickest paper or cardstock that you can. I've also made them on canvas, which looks great, too.

1. Start by writing the story or message. I find that typing it in a large typesize and printing it out makes it easier to hunt for the words.

2. Now hunt through your stash of magazines to find the right words. The type of paper is very important here: the thicker the better. Using weekly magazines is mostly a waste of time, as the paper is generally too thin and the glue seeps through. Cut out the words you need, using small, sharp scissors. Try to use as many different colors and fonts as you can and make sure the words are more or less the same size.

3. On a piece of scrap paper, draw the outline of the shape you're going to fill. You can make Word Arts in any shape, but I suggest a square or a rectangle to start with. If you're making a circular one, draw around a small plate or saucer.

4. Lay your cut-out words out in this spare shape to work out where they're going to go. If you then need to add or remove words from each line to make it all fit, you can do so without getting in a sticky mess.

5. Draw the outline of the shape very faintly on watercolor paper.

6. Place the two pieces of paper side by side: on the left, all the cut-out words and on the right, the watercolor paper. Taking one line at a time, paint a thin line of glue all the way across the shape and then one by one, using pliers or tweezers, pick up the words from the left-hand shape and stick them down.

7. Leave to dry, then very carefully rub out any pencil marks that are still visible. Place your artwork in a frame, ready to hang.

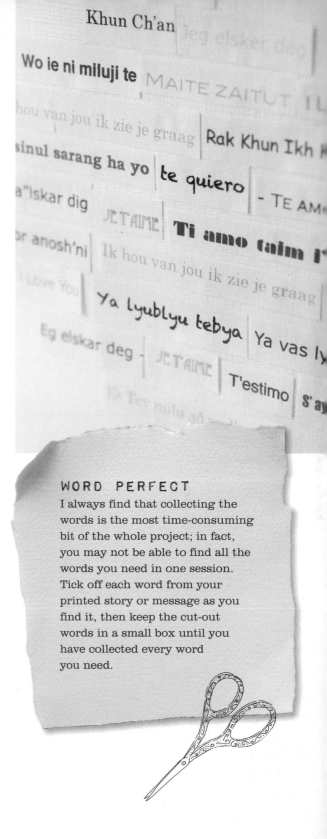

**WORD PERFECT**
I always find that collecting the words is the most time-consuming bit of the whole project; in fact, you may not be able to find all the words you need in one session. Tick off each word from your printed story or message as you find it, then keep the cut-out words in a small box until you have collected every word you need.

# ribbon pinboard

My kitchen would feel very empty without my pinboard. My life would also be a lot more disorganized. Anything remotely important gets stuck on the board in the hope that, as I walk past it a thousand times a day, I take note and do something about it.

These fabric-covered pinboards, with ribbon slats to hold shopping lists, reminders, and photos in place, are a little fiddly to make, but they are worth the effort and are bound to end up as a focal point of any room you hang them in. You can use any kind of board for this project. I used the back of an old picture frame, but corkboard would work well, too.

1. Cut out the fabric: it should be about 2 in. (5 cm) larger all around than the board. Place it right side down on your work surface and apply double-sided tape to all four edges of the fabric on the wrong side.

2. Peel the backing paper off the double-sided tape. Carefully center the board on the fabric.

3. Fold each corner of the fabric inward to form a triangle; the tip should just touch the edge of the board.

4. Working one side at a time, fold the edges of the fabric over the board as tightly and smoothly as you can. Press down firmly so that the fabric sticks to the double-sided tape. If you have a staple gun, fire staples into the board to hold the fabric in place.

5. Wrap a length of ribbon diagonally across the right side of the board from corner to corner. Fix the ends of the ribbon in place on the back of the board with drawing pins. Repeat across the opposite diagonal. Where the ribbons cross in the middle of your board, you can secure with a drawing pin if you wish. Repeat several times in each direction, until you have a criss-cross pattern of ribbon.

## INGREDIENTS

- BOARD
- FABRIC TO COVER THE BOARD
- DOUBLE-SIDED TAPE
- DRAWING PINS (THUMB TACKS)
- STAPLE GUN AND STAPLES (OPTIONAL)
- ABOUT 4 YD (4 M) RIBBON

### SPACING
It's entirely up to you how far apart you space the ribbons, but try to keep the distances between them even so that you get evenly sized diamonds.

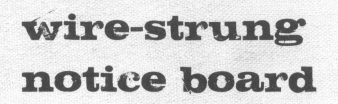

# wire-strung notice board

My picture frames all seem to be collapsing. I've tried gluing and tying them back together, but if this doesn't work, rather than throw them out I turn them into notice boards.

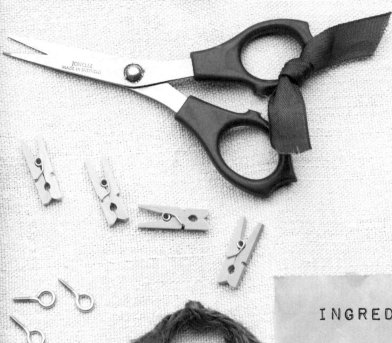

## INGREDIENTS

- WOODEN PICTURE FRAME
- TAPE MEASURE OR RULE
- PENCIL
- AWL (BRADAWL)
- SCREW EYES
- PICTURE CORD OR WIRE
- MINI WOODEN PEGS

My cupboards are full of so many pretty cards and letters, old photos and memories just waiting to be looked at, so this is an original way to have them pegged out on show. It's just like a pin board, but one where you need to be slightly more selective about what goes up. I like to treat it as an artwork full of possibilities.

MORE WIRES,
MORE TREASURES!
I have made this noticeboard with four strings, but feel free to make it with as many or as few as you like. The more strings you have, the more treasures you can add.

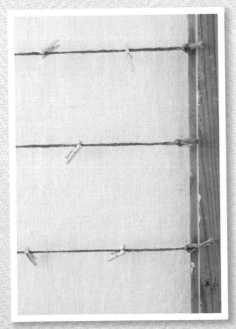

1. Decide how many wires you are going to have running along the frame. Each wire will need two screw eyes. Work out how far apart you want the wires to be and make a light pencil mark on each side of the frame at this point. Press the tip of an awl (bradawl) onto each marked point in turn and twist to begin creating the screw hole.

2. Carefully screw in the screw eyes on each side of the frame.

3. Thread a length of picture cord or wire into the first screw eye. Tie the cord securely, or twist the ends of the wire together tightly. Take the cord or wire across to the opposite screw hole and secure in the same way, making sure that it is pulled taut. Repeat until you have attached all the wires.

4. You are now ready to start hanging your special mementoes from the wires, using mini pegs to keep them in place.

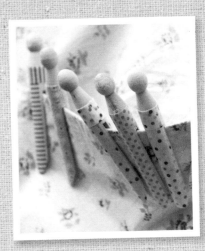

# to use
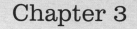

I am a firm believer that, no matter how useful something must be, it can also be beautiful. Why should a cup of tea sit on an old coaster or clothes hang from boring wire coat hangers?

This chapter shows how it takes very few tools and minimum effort to transform mundane everyday necessities into original, life-enhancing treasures that you'll want to show off to the world.

# fabric-covered notebooks

I came up with these to disguise a particularly hideous book about birds that had been sitting on my kitchen shelves for too long. In a crafting mood, I rummaged through my fabric supplies for a suitable remnant.

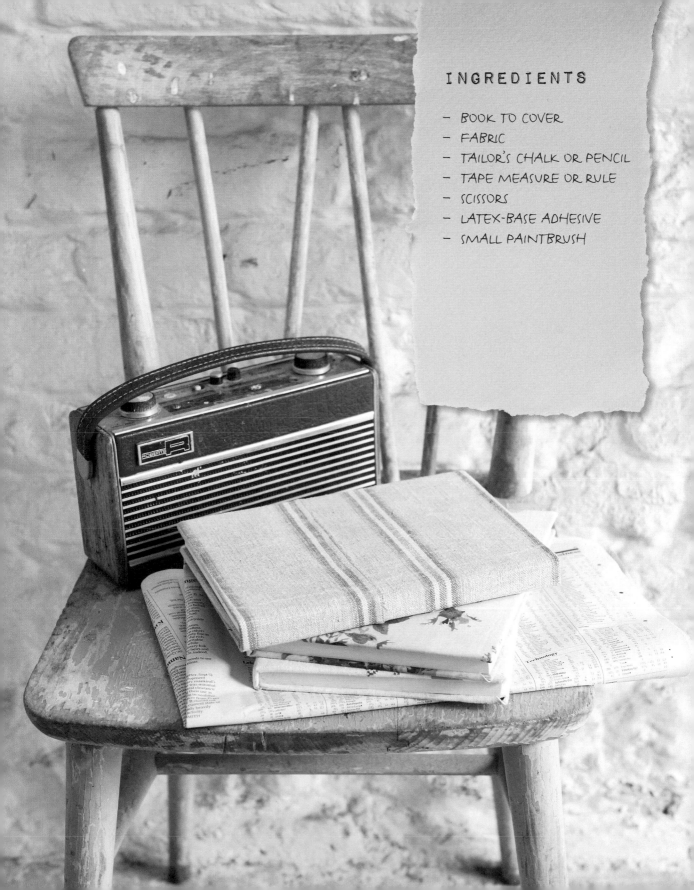

## INGREDIENTS

- BOOK TO COVER
- FABRIC
- TAILOR'S CHALK OR PENCIL
- TAPE MEASURE OR RULE
- SCISSORS
- LATEX-BASE ADHESIVE
- SMALL PAINTBRUSH

My first attempt wasn't great, but the new fabric jacket certainly looked more beautiful than the original book cover. It's taken me a long time to work out the best way to make these books look as professional as possible, but I think I've finally got it.

For me, the books are simply another way to show off beautiful fabric. I usually have about ten notebooks on the go at one time—diary, address book, recipe notebooks, and so on. I decided that if I'm going to be surrounded by these books all day, every day, I need them to be pretty as possible.

You can cover any hardback book you like. The joy is that you don't need much fabric at all.

1. Open the book, place it on the wrong side of the fabric, and draw around it with tailor's chalk or pencil, leaving at least 2 in. (5 cm) all around. Cut out.

2. Center the book on the wrong side of the fabric. Using a small paintbrush, paint a line of adhesive along the side edge of the inside front cover. Fold over the side edge, pressing the fabric down firmly to glue it in place. Repeat on the inside back cover, pulling the fabric tightly to keep things smooth.

3. Fold each corner down in a neat triangle and stick it down with a dab of glue. Holding the book closed, snip a slit in the fabric on either side of the top and bottom of the spine, cutting right up to the edge of the book. Cut a right-angle triangle to the side of each slit, as shown.

4. Using the paintbrush, paint a line of adhesive along the top and bottom edges of the front and back covers. Fold over the fabric and press in place, as before, pulling the fabric tightly to keep everything smooth.

5 You're now left with two squares of fabric running off the spine of the book. Dab a tiny bit of glue on the end of each square and, using the tip of your scissors, push the fabric down inside the book spine.

6 Apply glue to the folded-over fabric along the top, side, and bottom edges of the inside front cover, then fold back the first one or two pages of the notebook and press down to hide any messy fabric edges. Repeat on the inside back cover.

### NEAT AND TIDY

I usually stick down two pages on both the front and back to make everything as smooth and professional as possible. If this still doesn't look neat enough, glue in a piece of cardstock. You will need to cut it slightly smaller all around than the cover in order to close the book neatly.

# lavender-scented bath salts

No one ever believes these bath salts are homemade, which is weirdly satisfying. They make the most gorgeous present (if you can bear to give them away). This particular recipe is for lavender sleep salts, but you can experiment with different flavors by blending a few oils and botanicals here and there, like a proper alchemist.

## INGREDIENTS

- ONE CUP OF EPSOM SALTS
- HALF A CUP OF COARSE SALT OR SEA SALT
- QUARTER OF A CUP OF BAKING SODA
- 25 DROPS OF LAVENDER ESSENTIAL OIL
- SPRIGS OF DRIED LAVENDER FLOWERS
- MASON OR KILNER JAR, OR SIMILAR
- RIBBON
- LUGGAGE TAG

If you're going to give these away as a present, the packaging is obviously very important. Given the choice, I would use an old glass jar: mason or kilner jars work well. If you need to cart them on your travels, a lighter option is to use clear plastic gift bags. I buy mine in the bakery section of the supermarket.

### Essential oil safety

Essential oils are very strong. If you have a skin condition, are pregnant, have epilepsy or asthma, are taking a course of prescribed medication, or are in any doubt about any condition you may have, seek the advice of a doctor or aromatherapy practitioner before using them. Always keep essential oils out of the reach of children.

1  Mix all the salts and baking soda together in a large bowl.

2  Add the drops of lavender oil to the bowl and mix again.

3  Add as many sprigs of dried lavender as you want. Some people don't like having tiny bits of lavender floating around in the bathtub; if this is the case, use larger sprigs that will be easier to fish out.

4  Pour the bath salts into a jar. Find some pretty ribbon to tie in a bow around the jar. Neatly hand write the name and ingredients of your creation on a brown paper luggage tag, then tie the tag onto the ribbon.

## Rose salts

If you want something to perk you up in the morning, rather than wind you down, my other favorite concoction is rose salts. Swap the lavender sprigs for dried rose petals and the lavender essential oil for rose oil. If you're feeling extravagant, the crème de la crème of rose oils is pure Rose Otto oil.

It's very easy to make your own dried rose petals if you have an airing cupboard. Spread the rose petals out on a tray and leave overnight. Darker-colored petals seem to dry the best.

# découpaged fabric coat hangers

Every time I'm given coat hangers, I always assume they've been pulled out of a present drawer in a last-minute panic. They're not something I ever really got excited about, until recently. I think it was owning my first home that did it. We were so short of art works that I'd use clothes as decoration; I'd keep vintage petticoats on covered hangers and hang them on the wall.

## INGREDIENTS

- FABRIC
- SCISSORS
- WOODEN COAT HANGER
- PVA GLUE, WATERED DOWN SLIGHTLY
- SMALL PAINTBRUSH
- RIBBON TO DECORATE

1. Cut the fabric into small pieces; they don't need to be neat at all.

2. Paint the PVA and water mix onto the hanger a small bit at a time and stick down bits of the fabric, overlapping them slightly and painting over the top of the fabric as you go. Make sure no wood is left showing through.

3. Continue until you've covered the whole hanger, front and back.

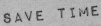

### SAVE TIME
Cut the fabric you're going to use into small bits before you start. This will also mean you get less sticky not having to alternate between cutting and sticking every two seconds.

4. Tie a small piece of ribbon or a strip of the fabric you used to cover the hanger in a bow and glue it to the front of the hanger, just below the hook.

5. Leave the glue to dry completely before hanging anything from the hanger.

# heatproof kitchen coasters

This is another project that I am almost too embarrassed to include in the book: these coasters are so simple that I'm sure even my two-year-old Cub could make them. You can probably make one in under a minute.

Despite this, I really would be lost without them—and my new and very gorgeous kitchen table would not look so beautiful. They are both incredibly useful and pretty—people always ask me about them, so here they are.

You can, of course, make these with any old tiles, but that kind of defeats the object: they're meant to be a thing of beauty as well as utilitarian, and I didn't have in mind some boring kitchen tile that you might find at your local home improvements store! Look in antique stores and markets for vintage, one-of-a-kind tiles.

1. Cut the felt to the same size as the tile.

2. Apply superglue to the back of the tile and stick on the felt, carefully smoothing it out with your fingers.

3. Leave to dry—et voilà! Now you have your very own heatproof tile, ready and waiting to protect your tabletop.

# INGREDIENTS

- TILES—THE MORE
  UNUSUAL AND
  BEAUTIFUL THE BETTER
- FELT
- SCISSORS
- SUPERGLUE

# fabric pouches

I have a real tendency to hoard things. I never throw anything away because I know that, after a few months, I will have changed my mind and decide that I actually rather like it and want it back. This magpie habit means that I have a lot of stuff. I even have things that I'm not quite sure what I'm ever going to do with—broken bits of jewelry, vintage pots once filled with lip gloss, ribbons, and odd buttons—things that most people would consider to be rubbish.

Despite the clutter habit, I'm not a fan of mess. I started making these little pouches so I that I could round up all the bits and bobs that didn't have a home and keep everything tidy(ish). (I say "-ish," as a tidy house with a two-year-old Cub is practically impossible.)

I don't tend to follow a pattern for the pouches. I'm more guided by the size of the fabric that I've chosen to use. I then make one of two shapes—either an envelope style with a fold-over top or a super-simple drawstring one.

## Drawstring jewelry pouch

I tend to use a drawstring pouch to store my treasures in at home. If I'm away from home and want to take only a few bits and pieces of jewelry with me, I use the envelope pouch (shown on page 94)—perfect for slipping in the bottom of my suitcase and keeping things straight and tangle free.

1. Cut your fabric to the required size. The piece I've used here measures 21 x 10 in. (53.5 x 25 cm).

2. Along each long edge, fold over ¼ in. (5 mm) to the wrong side and press with your fingertips, then fold over another ¼ in. (5 mm) and pin in place. Machine stitch, or backstitch by hand.

3. Along each short edge, fold over ¼ in. (5 mm) to the wrong side and press with your fingertips, then fold over another ½ in. (12 mm) and pin in place. Machine stitch, or backstitch by hand, sewing as close to the edge as possible; this forms a channel for the drawstring.

4   Fold the fabric in half lengthwise, right sides together, and pin along the sides.

5   Machine or hand stitch along the sides of the pouch, stopping just below the stitching line of the drawstring channel. Turn right side out and press the pouch on the right side.

6   Feed ribbon or cotton tape through the channel at the top of the pouch.

## WATERPROOF POUCH

To use a drawstring pouch as a wash bag or even as something to carry around wet swimwear in, simply sew in some waterproof fabric as a lining.

SCALE UP
If you scale these up to a larger size, they are gorgeous to keep your favorite or very fragile clothes in when you travel.

INGREDIENTS

- MAIN AND LINING FABRICS
- SCISSORS
- TAILOR'S CHALK OR FABRIC MARKER PEN
- PINS
- SEWING MACHINE OR NEEDLE AND THREAD
- SMALL BUTTON

# Envelope-style pouch

The button on the flap of this pouch is just for show, to avoid the fiddly business of making a buttonhole. However, you could attach a snap fastener or pieces of hook-and-loop tape to the underside of the flap and the front of the pouch if you want a secure fastening.

1. Cut a piece of fabric and a piece of lining fabric to the required size. The pieces I've used here measure 12¼ x 8 in. (31 x 20 cm).

2. On both pieces, mark the center of one short end. On the wrong side of the fabric, using tailor's chalk or a fabric marker pen, draw a line from the center point to 4¾ in. (12 cm) along each long side. Cut along the lines so that you have a triangular-shaped tip; this will be the flap of the pouch.

3. Pin the main fabric and lining pieces right sides together. Taking a ⅜-in. (1-cm) seam, machine stitch all around, leaving a 3-in. (8-cm) gap in the center of the straight short end. Turn right side out and press.

4. Turn the edges of the gap under and whipstitch to close.

5. Stitch a button to the right side of the flap, close to the tip.

# ribbon-trimmed Panama hat

I love a good hat. I'd like to be slightly braver and wear them more often, but for some reason I often feel a bit self-conscious. Panama hats are an exception, though. In France, from May to October, they became part of our everyday wardrobe. Getting up each morning, on would go the dress, the flip-flops, the factor 50, and the Panama. After a while, however, I got a bit bored with the standard black trim, so I thought I'd experiment with something different.

## INGREDIENTS

- PANAMA HAT
- TAPE MEASURE
- FABRIC, RIBBON, OR OTHER READY-MADE TRIM
- PINS
- NEEDLE AND MATCHING THREAD

As well as my obsession with all things faded and floral, I have a real weakness for anything old and Indian orientated. The New Year after we got married, we went to Goa for a couple of weeks. The biggest lure for me was spending hours trawling the markets for antique treasures. I came home laden with vintage sari trims, beaded bags from the Banjara tribes, and more cowrie-shell tassels than I know what to do with.

So when I was looking to replace the standard black band on my Panama hat, I headed straight for my stash of vintage sari trims. It was a match made in heaven: even Philip Treacy might be impressed.

If you're using a real, genuine Panama hat, be careful not to get it wet as they shrink dramatically right before your eyes. I have a whole wall full of them that are too small for even the Cub to wear after incidents at sea...

It is easy to customize these hats, although it can be quite fiddly. I always think I can finish one off and be poolside in about ten minutes flat, but in reality it takes slightly longer. Allow yourself an hour for your first go.

## CHOOSING A TRIM

When I make these to sell, striped ticking fabric and antique grainsacks are always the most popular with men.

If you want to keep it as simple as possible, use some ribbon so that you don't even need to decide how thick to make the band. Gros-grain (petersham) ribbon works gorgeously.

Hunt for vintage cotton lace trims: somehow they always seem to be the perfect width.

If you're cutting your new band from fabric, cut it the same depth as the original hat band (if you don't mind raw edges) or add about ¾ in. (2 cm) to allow for folding the raw edges under if you want a neat finish.

1. Unpick the original band from the hat. Measure the circumference of the hat at the point where the trim will go and add 2 in. (5 cm) or so.

2. If you've cut your new hat band from fabric and want neat edges, fold under the long raw edges by ⅜ in. (1 cm) and press. This is not necessary with ready-made ribbons and trims. However, I quite like the look of raw edges; it's entirely up to you!

3. Arrange your chosen trim on the hat, folding the raw edges under, and pin it in place, overlapping the ends.

4. Thread a sewing needle with thread to match the color of the trim. Every 2–3 in. (5–8 cm), sew the band down. The needle doesn't have to go through the straw: with a bit of persuasion, you can coax it through the weave of the hat, in between the lengths of straw, and up through the trim again.

6. When the band is secure, you're ready to hit the beach!

## DISGUISING THE JOIN

The join between the two ends of the trim is often quite obvious, so you may want to make a little wrap of fabric to hide it.

Cut a length of fabric slightly less than twice the depth of the finished trim and about 1 in. (2.5 cm) wide. Fold the long edges to the wrong side and press, then loop the fabric over the top and bottom of the trim. Catch the top and bottom of the loop in with your stitches when you sew the band in place. I think these loops look best placed on the side of the hat, in the middle.

HEAVYDUTY GLUE
If you don't have a glue gun,
use a mix of superglue and
latex-base adhesive: better to
be safe than sorry.

# pom-pom paniers

The fleur-de-lis may be the symbol of France, but to me the symbol of Provence is a panier—a straw basket. Having lived in France, I realize that the panier is a way of life. The French use them for shopping, for beach bags, for storage, to collect figs and lavender... There's something so wholesome and comforting about them: they're neither flashy nor shiny and there's not a logo in sight.

## INGREDIENTS

- TAPE MEASURE
- STRAW BASKET
- POM-POM TRIM
- SCISSORS
- GLUE GUN (OR A MIX OF SUPERGLUE AND LATEX-BASE ADHESIVE, PLUS A SMALL PAINTBRUSH)
- EMBROIDERY NEEDLE AND STRANDED EMBROIDERY FLOSS (THREAD)—OPTIONAL

I first made a pom-pom basket after I mistakenly took someone else's home from the beach. I realized the only way to stop it happening again would be to make mine stand out. I've always loved pom-poms, so decided the combination would be a match made in heaven. They are easy to make—slightly fiddly, but nothing taxing. Choose any trim you like but make it as light as you can, because gravity is not on your side. I have had a few weightier pom-poms coming unstuck after only a few outings, take the time to glue each little bit well and truly down.

1. Measure around the outside of the top of the basket, add an extra 1–2 in. (2.5–5 cm) to this measurement, and cut a piece of pom-pom trim to this length.

2. There is always a little messy area on the basket where the maker has had to cut the straw. Start at this point. I apply glue over about 4 in. (10 cm) of the basket rim at a time and glue the trim down bit by bit. Keep going until you've applied pom-pom trim all the way around.

3. When you get to the end, you will have a bit of pom-pom trim left over. Snip off the pom-poms, so that you're left with just the ribbon part, then fold the end under for a neat finish. Leave it for as long as you can, until the glue is completely dry.

4. To make doubly sure that the pom-poms stay in place, thread an embroidery needle with stranded embroidery floss (thread) and work a few cross stitches, or straight stitches on the diagonal, through the ribbon. The needle doesn't have to go through the straw: with a bit of persuasion, you can coax it through the weave of the basket, in between the lengths of straw. This looks so pretty if you choose a brightly colored thread to contrast with the pom-poms.

# fabric bracelets

Everyone likes a swanky jewel—a bit of gold or some
sort of sparkling, precious stone. But sometimes, you
just want something simple and inexpensive that you
don't need to worry about. These bracelets definitely
fall into the latter category, and are loved by both
tiny people and grown-ups alike.

## INGREDIENTS

- TAPE MEASURE
- LIBERTY LAWN
  COTTON FABRIC
- SCISSORS
- BEADS OR BUTTONS
- NEEDLE AND LINEN
  THREAD

The fabric bracelets shown here are made using Liberty lawn cotton. It is so lightweight and soft, which makes braiding (plaiting) much easier; the bracelets also sit better on the wrist.

You can thread as many or as few beads on as you like. I've even made some without anything except the fabric and they look divine—simple and understated...

This is not the kind of project where I will tell you to put one bead here and one bead there—it all comes down to your personal taste and how you want your bracelet to look.

①  Measure the circumference of your wrist and double it. Cut three strips of fabric to this length and ½ in. (12 mm) wide.

②  Hold the strips together in a bunch and tie a knot at one end. Start braiding (plaiting) the fabric. When you reach the point at which you want a bead, thread one onto one of the strands of fabric. To attach a button, or a bead with a hole too small to feed the fabric through it, thread a needle with a short length of matching thread and stitch the bead or button in place.

3. Continue braiding the strips, adding beads wherever you choose.

4. Finish by tying the three strands together in a knot at the end.

## FINISHING FLOURISH

I have a real thing about alphabet beads and love making necklaces with them, spelling out phrases and names. Children always love having them with their names on. You can get them in almost any craft store, and eBay and Amazon both have a huge supply in many different colors and shapes.

Recently, I've started adding little silver and gold crimp beads, which stop the larger beads from slipping around and make everything look a lot more professional. Before you start threading on your alphabet beads, thread a crimp bead onto the cord or stringing material at the point where you want the first bead to sit, then squeeze the bead with flat-nose pliers to tighten it in place. Do the same thing when you've threaded on all the alphabet beads.

# pretty pins

Everyone uses clothespins for something or other. They are one of life's necessities that just sit there, inoffensively minding their own business—but being unavoidably quite dull. I decided to give mine a makeover and now they hang out on my windowsill, in pride of place, looking beauteous.

## INGREDIENTS

- — TAPE MEASURE OR RULER
- — WOODEN CLOTHESPINS
- — WASHI TAPE
- — SCISSORS

## QUICK COLOR

If you want to make these with children, a slightly easier and less fiddly idea is simply to paint or color the pegs with felt-tipped pens.

I've covered them with washi tape, a decorative masking tape from Japan. I don't know what I did before this tape was available. I use it every day for something or other—on beautiful gift wrapping, to label jars of homemade jam, to stick books back together, even to make pretty notecards.

My clothespins are the rounded, old-fashioned type, but you can use the easier-to-find flat square ones, too. These are actually much easier to decorate, as there are no curved sides. You never know, clothespins like this might even make hanging up the washing more enjoyable.

## ADDED SPARKLE

If you want something a little more glitzy, Swarovski crystals are fab. Just glue them on in lines, one by one, using a strong glue. If you have some mini pliers to hand it'll make picking up the crystals a hundred times easier.

① Roughly measure the length of the clothespin, starting from below the bobble on the top.

② Cut some washi tape to the same length. Stick the tape in the middle of the wooden clothespin, between the slits, as smoothly and evenly as you can. Using sharp scissors, trim the tape level with the clothespin. Repeat on the opposite side.

③ Cut another length of tape about 3 in. (7.5 cm) long, and wrap it once or twice around the top of the clothespin, just below the bobble, to complete.

# INGREDIENTS

- TAPE MEASURE
- COAT HANGER
- FABRIC
- SCISSORS
- PINS
- NEEDLE AND THREAD
- SEWING MACHINE
  (OPTIONAL)
- RIBBON OR TWINE
  TO DECORATE

# clothespin bag

This project goes hand in hand with the previous one. Obviously, I couldn't keep my gorgeous new pins in a grotty old bag—so out came the sewing machine...

Granted, this is not an especially exciting project—but seeing the beautiful fabric swinging from the washing line every day really does lift the spirits. To borrow William Morris's famous dictum, you should have nothing in your home that you do not know to be useful or believe to be beautiful.

Throw in some decorated clothespins, too, and this would make a perfect gift for any domestic goddess.

1. Measure the width of your coat hanger and add ¾ in. (2 cm).

2. Cut three rectangles of fabric—one for the back measuring 13 x 20 in. (33 x 50 cm) and the other two (which will overlap each over and form the front of the bag) measuring 8 x 20 in. (20 x 50 cm).

3. Fold over ⅜ in. (1 cm) and then another ⅜ in (1 cm) along one short end of each of the smaller pieces of fabric, pin in place, and machine stitch.

4. Place the fabric for the back of the bag right side up on your work surface. Place the two pieces for the front of the bag right side down on top, aligning the raw edges and with the hemmed edges overlapping each other.

5. Pin and baste (tack) the panels together all around the outside edge. Stitching ⅜ in. (1 cm) from the edge, machine stitch around the outside edge (or backstitch, by hand). Turn the bag right side out.

6. Using sharp scissors, cut a neat slit about 2 in. (5 cm) long at the center top of the bag. Feed the hook of the coat hanger through the slit you have just cut.

7. Wrap ribbon or twine around the coat hanger hook to decorate.

### RECYCLE
An easy option is to use an old shirt or T-shirt, instead of a pretty chintz fabric, to make the bag: simply slip it over the coat hanger and then create your shape.

# linen tote bag

Not that I'm trying to put you off making one, but these bags are probably the trickiest to make of all my projects. You need to be able to cut and follow a proper pattern, as they do demand accurate measurements. It took me a couple of attempts, but once I'd got the hang of it I couldn't stop making them.

## INGREDIENTS

- PATTERNS ON PAGES 172–173
- NEWSPAPER TO MAKE PATTERNS
- PAPER AND FABRIC SCISSORS
- 43½ X 27½ IN. (110 X 70 CM) FABRIC FOR THE OUTSIDE OF THE BAG
- 43½ X 27½ IN. (110 X 70 CM) COTTON FABRIC FOR LINING
- NEEDLE AND THREAD
- SEWING MACHINE
- IRON

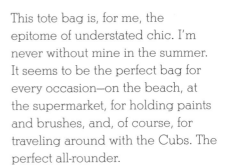

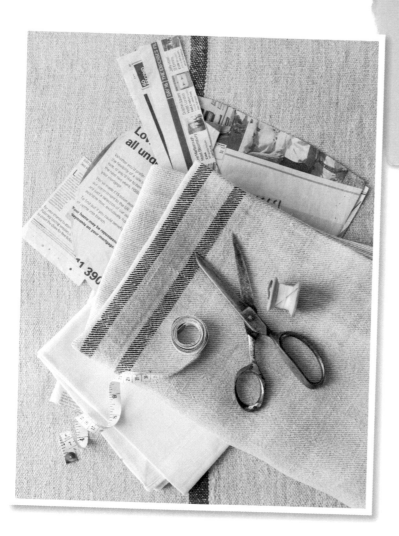

This tote bag is, for me, the epitome of understated chic. I'm never without mine in the summer. It seems to be the perfect bag for every occasion—on the beach, at the supermarket, for holding paints and brushes, and, of course, for traveling around with the Cubs. The perfect all-rounder.

I've always made them in some kind of linen or grain sack, for the appearance as much as for the durability of the fabric. The more hardwearing a fabric, the longer it will last you. Of course, you could easily use a flimsier chintz and it would look ravishing; it just won't be as practical for carrying the groceries home.

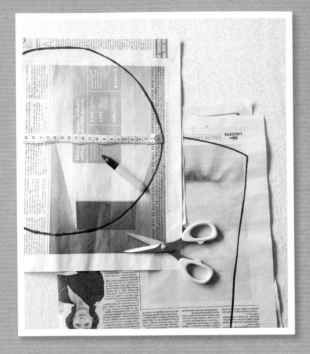

1. Enlarge the patterns on pages 172–173 by the percentages specified, trace onto newspaper, add a ⅜-in. (1-cm) seam allowance all around each piece, and cut out.

2. Pin your paper patterns onto the relevant fabrics and cut out. Cut two side pieces, two straps, and one base piece from the main fabric, and two side pieces, two straps, one base piece, and one pocket from the lining fabric.

3. With right sides together, pin and baste (tack) the two outer side pieces together. Remove the pins. Machine stitch the sides, then remove the basting (tacking) stitches. Finish the seams by overlocking the edges; if your machine does not do overlocking, zigzag stitch close to the edge. Repeat with the two lining side pieces.

**4** With right sides together, pin and baste (tack) the outer fabric base piece to the outer bag sides. Remove the pins. Machine stitch, then remove the basting (tacking) stitches. As in step 3, overlock or zigzag stitch the edges to finish the seams. Turn the bag right side out and press. Repeat with the lining.

**5** Turn each edge of each strap to the wrong side by ¼ in. (5 mm), press, and pin in place. Place one main fabric and one lining fabric strap wrong sides together and machine stitch all around, stitching close to the edge. Remove the pins.

**6** If you wish, hem the raw edges of the pocket; I prefer to leave the pockets unhemmed, but it's entirely up to you. With the wrong side of the pocket against the right side of the lining, pin and baste (tack) the pocket to the middle of the lining. Remove the pins. Machine stitch around the sides and base of the pocket, ⅜ in. (1 cm) from the edge. Remove the basting (tacking) stitches.

**7** Turn the top of the bag over to the wrong side by ⅝ in. (1.5 cm) and press. Pin and baste (tack). Repeat with the lining.

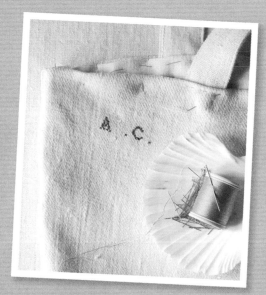

**8** With wrong sides together, slot the lining inside the main bag and pin together at the top, all the way around.

**9** Work out where you want the straps to be and then pin them in between the outer bag and the lining, positioning the end of each strap 1 in. (2.5 cm) down from the top of the bag. Baste (tack) the straps in place. Machine stitch all around the top of the bag, then work another line of stitching just below the first for extra security.

# matchbox covers

Matches are definitely one of life's necessities. Most of the time they come in hideous orange boxes, which is my worst color of all time. We have a real thing about fires and light one even when it's a warm spring or fall day. We order our logs on September 1st and keep them coming until at least April. For this reason, we have a stash of matchboxes dotted all over the house— on the mantelpiece, on kitchen surfaces, on hall tables, and stored in drawers. Needless to say, they don't hang around for long before I give them a bit of a makeover.

There really are no rules when it comes to making these. My one piece of advice is to give yourself as good a base to work with as possible. Take time to cover the existing patterns with some thick, brown parcel paper; if you want a very easy job, sticky labels are magic. You then have a blank canvas to work with and you can get carried away creating beautiful patterns rather than worrying about strategically placing things to hide what's underneath.

### Decoration ideas

Obviously it's up to you to decide how you want to decorate, but here are some ideas to get you started:

Newspaper, glitter, buttons, old maps, old postcards, vintage cigarette cards, old seed packets, beads, washi tape, vintage comics, photos.

## INGREDIENTS

- MATCHBOX
- PENCIL AND RULER
- BROWN PARCEL PAPER OR STICKY LABELS
- SCISSORS
- PVA GLUE AND SMALL PAINTBRUSH, OR
- DOUBLE-SIDED TAPE
- DECORATION OF YOUR CHOICE

1. Measure the top, side, and base of the matchbox and cut a piece of brown paper to this size.

2. Cover the top, side, and base with a thin layer of glue or double-sided tape and carefully stick the brown paper in place, smoothing it out with your fingers to make sure there are no wrinkles. Alternatively, use a large sticky label.

3. Decorate the matchbox as you wish, making sure you cover all the brown paper.

# worry dolls

I am a big worrier—always have been, probably always will be. I can vividly remember being given my first little box of Guatemalan worry dolls. It was like being given a small miracle and I truly believed that they took my worries away. Each night I would tell them what was on my mind, tuck them under my pillow, and then wake up without a care in the world the next day. It takes rather more than a little doll to solve my worries these days, but I like to hope these might help someone.

## INGREDIENTS

- QUICK-DRYING GLUE
- SMALL PAINTBRUSH
- SMALL WOODEN BEADS TO USE AS THE HEADS
- WOODEN TOOTHPICKS
- EMBROIDERY FLOSS (THREAD) IN LOTS OF COLORS
- SCISSORS
- FELT-TIPPED PENS (OPTIONAL)

I started making these dolls with the much younger me in mind. Twenty years ago, I would have gone crazy for them—and even as a grown-up, I still love them; they look adorable and sit like quiet friends on our mantelpiece. I really enjoy making them and they're so easy that anyone with a bit of patience will be able to create them, too. Even Chaz (quite) enjoys joining in; he actually made half of the ones shown here.

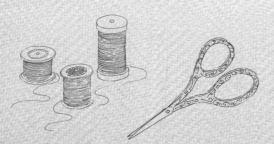

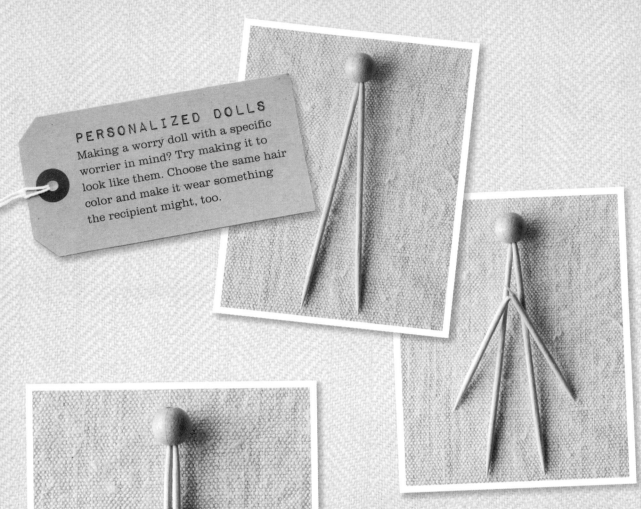

**PERSONALIZED DOLLS**
Making a worry doll with a specific
worrier in mind? Try making it to
look like them. Choose the same hair
color and make it wear something
the recipient might, too.

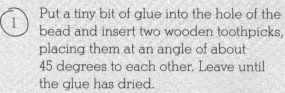

(1) Put a tiny bit of glue into the hole of the
bead and insert two wooden toothpicks,
placing them at an angle of about
45 degrees to each other. Leave until
the glue has dried.

(2) Snap a toothpick in half to use as the arms
and place it about one-third of the way
down the body. You don't need to glue the
arms down, as they will be held in place
by the floss (thread) in the next step.

(3) Cut a length of embroidery floss (thread)
and begin winding it around the
toothpicks, covering the bend of the arms.

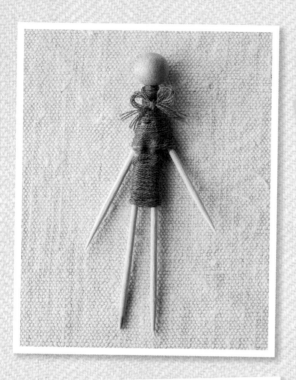

## BOY DOLL

If you want a boy worry doll, stop wrapping the floss (thread) around when the sweater reaches "waist" length. Cut off the floss and apply a tiny dab of glue to hold the end in place. Starting at the "ankles" with a new color of floss and working upward, wrap the floss around one leg at a time to make the pants. Again, secure the end with a dab of glue.

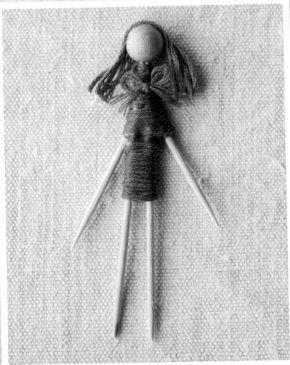

4) This is where you make the doll's clothes. Give her a bow tie, a long dress, long sleeves, a really glitzy dress with metallic thread—anything you like. Just keep wrapping floss (thread) around until you reach the desired length. Secure the end of the floss with a tiny dab of glue.

5) To make the hair, cut the floss (thread) to the length you want and stick it onto the bead with a few dabs of glue.

6) I prefer my dolls to be faceless, but if you wish you can draw a face with felt-tipped pens. Before you do so, test the pens on a spare bead to make sure that the ink won't run.

# secret book

I think the idea for this book stemmed from when I was little and needed to hide my favorite girly trinkets from my two hooligan brothers. I've never seen another one like it in real life, although I know that big companies have made metal versions that can be used like a safety deposit box.

I've covered this book in one of my favorite fabrics, so to anyone looking along my shelves it just looks like one of my usual fabric notebooks—just a bit fatter than normal. You can, of course, use any size of book you want, but obviously the thicker the book, the more things you can hide inside it.

If you're going to cover the book as well as cut out the pages, it'll make life a lot easier if the book is hard backed. If you're not especially bothered about giving it a fabric jacket, you could easily use a little paperback book and just store your credit cards and secret love letters inside.

# INGREDIENTS

- PENCIL
- RULER
- LARGE HARDBACK BOOK
- SHARP SCALPEL OR UTILITY KNIFE
- PVA GLUE
- SMALL PAINTBRUSH
- COLORED PAPER OR THIN CARDSTOCK
- SCISSORS
- FABRIC FOR THE JACKET (OPTIONAL)
- LATEX-BASE ADHESIVE (IF YOU ARE MAKING A FABRIC JACKET)

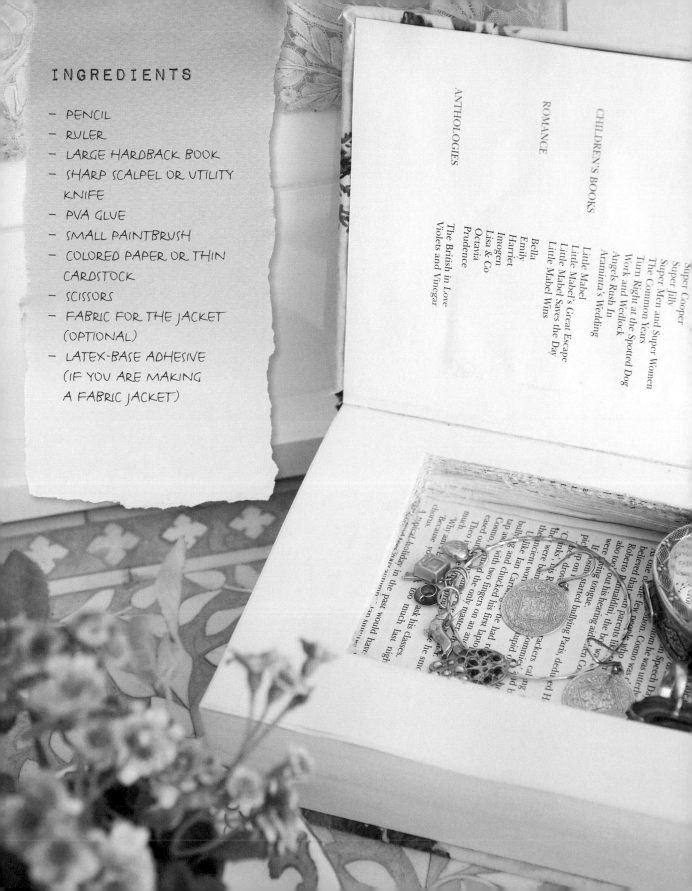

## CHILDREN'S BOOKS

Super Cooper
Super Jilly
Super Men and Super Women
The Common Years
Turn Right at the Spotted Dog
Work and Wedlock
Angels Rush In
Araminta's Wedding
Little Mabel
Little Mabel's Great Escape
Little Mabel Saves the Day
Little Mabel Wins

## ROMANCE

Bella
Emily
Harriet
Imogen
Lisa & Co
Octavia
Prudence

## ANTHOLOGIES

The British in Love
Violets and Vinegar

1. Using a pencil and a ruler, mark out the size of the box you want to create on the first page of your book, making sure you leave a border at least ¾ in. (2 cm) wide all around.

2. Using a scalpel or a utility knife, follow your pencil markings and start to cut out the paper from the middle. Take your time and remember to be very careful with your scalpel or craft knife.

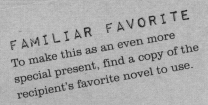

FAMILIAR FAVORITE
To make this as an even more special present, find a copy of the recipient's favorite novel to use.

3  When you've cut as deep a hole as you want, tidy up the edges. Mix PVA glue with water (about two-thirds glue and one-third water), then paint over the sides of the hole that you've cut to stick all the pages together. Leave until the glue has dried.

4  Cut four pieces of colored paper or thin cardstock the same size as a page of your book. Brush PVA glue over the endpapers at the front and back of the book, then stick the paper or cardstock in place. Leave until the glue has dried.

5  If you want to cover your secret book in fabric, follow the instructions for the fabric-covered notebooks on page 78.

# linen laundry bags

When we lived in France, I traveled back and forth to England every month or so. If my visit was just for a few days, I didn't want to waste precious time doing my laundry, so I would bring enough clothes to last and keep the worn ones at the bottom of my suitcase. When the Cub arrived, however, my organizational skills had to step up a few levels. I soon learned that flying with a baby in tow doesn't mean that you get more baggage allowance: my bag just became our bag.

I'd seen laundry bags in shops and always thought they were a bit of a waste of time—something to give "the person who has everything." Now I can't travel without at least two in my suitcase.

Being made from pillowcases, they really couldn't be easier to create as most of the work has already been done for you. I love using really old cases that I've found in antique shops. Look for ones with a wide border at one end and then all you need to do is add a few stitches.

1) Turn the pillowcase inside out and lay it on a flat surface. Turn the open end down by 4 in. (10 cm).

2) Baste (tack) the turned-down end all around, leaving a big enough space for the ribbon. Machine stitch as close to the edge of the turned-down end as possible. Remove the basting (tacking) stitches and turn the pillowcase right side out.

3) Cut a very small slit that is just slightly wider than the ribbon down one side of the turned-down section. Turn the raw edges of the slit under and then whipstitch to neaten them.

4) Attach a safety pin to one end of the ribbon and feed it all the way through the channel you've sewn until it comes at out the other side. This will be the drawstring.

5) You're now ready to start packing your bags!

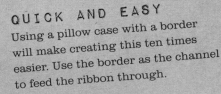

QUICK AND EASY
Using a pillow case with a border will make creating this ten times easier. Use the border as the channel to feed the ribbon through.

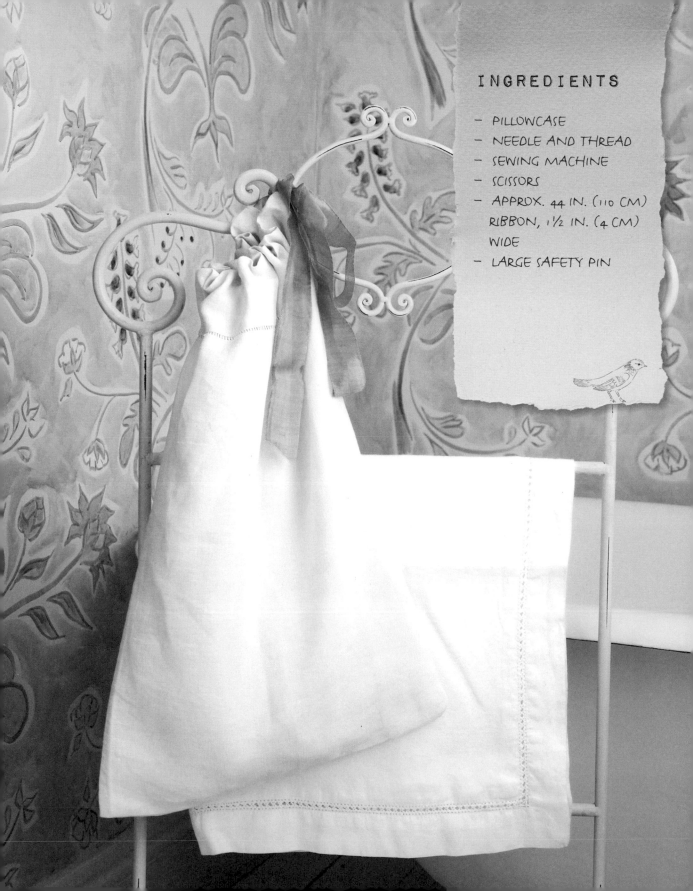

## INGREDIENTS

- PILLOWCASE
- NEEDLE AND THREAD
- SEWING MACHINE
- SCISSORS
- APPROX. 44 IN. (110 CM)
  RIBBON, 1½ IN. (4 CM)
  WIDE
- LARGE SAFETY PIN

# linen apron

Whenever I see an apron in a shop, I'm always amazed by how much it costs. Fair enough if they're made from super-swanky vintage linen—but more often than not, they're just functional cotton ones.

When Chaz and I first met, I could barely boil an egg and my staple diet was baked potato, beans, and cheese. He, on the other hand, has always been the most incredible cook and has slowly been sharing his wisdom with me. Nine years on and I am completely in love with everything about cooking and food.

Since I've developed this love affair with cooking, I've been spending rather a lot of time in an apron. Naturally I wanted a pretty one, so I delved into my fabric supplies to see what I could create. I like pockets in my aprons, but it's totally up to you. You may not want to bother with one at all.

This apron has proper straps, but I've also made them with ribbon ties, which is simpler and far less time consuming. And, of course, you can change the ribbons when they fray or you are bored with the color.

## INGREDIENTS

- NEWSPAPER FOR PATTERN
- FELT-TIPPED PEN
- 1 YD (1 M) MAIN FABRIC
- ½ YD (50 CM) CONTRAST FABRIC FOR WAIST TIES, NECK STRAP, AND POCKET
- PAPER AND FABRIC SCISSORS
- TAPE MEASURE
- SEWING MACHINE
- NEEDLE AND THREAD

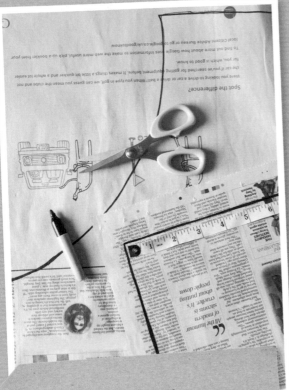

## EVEN CURVES

Place a dinner plate on the two marks and draw around the edge to get a smooth, even curve.

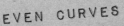

① Fold a large piece of newspaper in half and mark out a rectangle measuring 37½ x 12½ in. (95 x 32 cm). Make a mark approx. 6½ in. (17 cm) in from one short end and 15 in. (38 cm) down from the top edge, then join the two marks in a curved line to shape the sides of the apron. Cut along the drawn lines, then unfold the newspaper.

② For the waist ties, cut two rectangles of newspaper measuring 45 x 3 in. (114 x 8 cm). For the shoulder strap, cut a rectangle measuring 24½ x 3 in. (62 x 8 cm). For the pocket cut a rectangle measuring 14 x 12¼ in. (36 x 31 cm).

③ Pin the paper patterns on the relevant fabrics and cut out. I used a striped linen for the waist ties, neck strap, and pocket; make sure that you align the pattern with the stripes.

(4) Turn the top edge of the pocket over to the wrong side by ¾ in. (2 cm) and then by ¾ in. (2 cm) again, press, pin in place, and machine stitch. Then turn the other three edges over to the wrong side by ¾ in. (2 cm), press, and pin.

(5) Place the pocket right side up on the front of the apron. Pin, then baste (tack) it in place, using a contrasting color of thread. Remove the pins, machine stitch around the side and bottom edges, then remove the basting (tacking) stitches.

(6) Fold each waist tie and the neck strap in half lengthwise, right sides together, and pin. Baste (tack) along the long raw edge, using a contrasting color of thread. Remove the pins, then machine stitch along the one short end and the long raw edge, stitching ⅜ in. (1 cm). Remove the basting (tacking) stitches. Turn the ties and strap right side out and press, making sure the stitching line runs down the center back of the straps. Turn under the raw short end of each tie and press.

NEAT TURNS
Use a knitting needle or a chopstick to turn the straps right side out.

**7** Turn the top and bottom edges of the apron over to the wrong side by ⅜ in. (1 cm) and then again by 1½ in. (4 cm), and press. Turn the side edges over to the wrong side by ⅜ in. (1 cm) and then again by ¾ in. (2 cm), and press. Baste (tack), using a contrasting color of thread. Remove the pins, then machine stitch. Remove the basting (tacking) stitches.

**8** Pin the waist ties in position at the top of the straight section of each side of the apron, aligning the ends with the edge of the hem. Baste (tack) in place. Machine stitch across the width of the each tie, continue stitching around to form a square, then reinforce by machine stitching diagonally across the square in both directions. Remove the basting (tacking) stitches.

**9** Pin the right side of the neck strap to the wrong side of the top of the apron, with the ends of the strap 1 in. (2.5 cm) down from the top edge, and pin in place.

**10** Cut a 10 x 2½-in. (26 x 6-cm) rectangle of the main fabric. Fold the long sides under by ⅜ in. (1 cm) and press. With wrong sides together, place the rectangle along the top edge of the apron, on top of the neck strap. Fold the short ends under so that they're level with the apron sides, and pin in place. Machine stitch all around the rectangle, as close to the edge as possible, making sure you catch the neck strap in with the stitches.

# block print napkins

I think these came from my love for all things Indian. We are doing up our house as I write and, if I had my way, every wall and drape would be wearing a block-print pattern.

Block printing has been one of those things I've adored, but always presumed it was way beyond my crafting ability. Until now. I am well and truly hooked—although, of course, I haven't quite mastered it on a professional level and the prospect of layering the prints makes me slightly nervous.

I know there are ways of making homemade block prints by carving designs out of potatoes, but to get the intricate prints I was after, I had to splash out on some proper wooden blocks.

I've made napkins here, but obviously you can make anything you like. The only limit is how much fabric you have to play with. Tablecloths, window blinds, and an apron are next on my list. I've suggested using readymade napkins, but I actually found some old pieces of white linen in a market and cut them into pieces roughly the right size. I don't think it matters that they don't all match perfectly.

## INGREDIENTS

- FABRIC BLOCK-PRINT PAINTS
- PLATE OR PALETTE TO PUT THE PAINT ON
- WOODEN BLOCK PRINTS
- MINI ROLLER
- WHITE COTTON OR LINEN NAPKINS
- HOUSEHOLD (WHITE) SPIRIT TO CLEAN YOUR TOOLS

(1) Squeeze some paint out onto the plate or palette.

(2) Evenly cover the block print with paint by rolling it on with the mini roller. Before you stamp it onto the fabric, make sure that there are no lumps of paint or bits without paint.

**BE PATIENT!**
Don't do as I did and fold the napkins a few hours later: they will smudge. This paint takes far longer to dry than you think. Leave the napkins to dry for at least 24 hours.

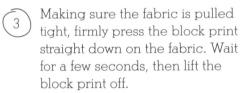

3. Making sure the fabric is pulled tight, firmly press the block print straight down on the fabric. Wait for a few seconds, then lift the block print off.

4. Repeat until you have done as many prints as you want and then hang the napkins up to dry somewhere well away from sticky fingers.

5. Clean the roller and palette with household (white) spirit.

## INGREDIENTS

- TERRACOTTA PLANT POTS
- CHALKBOARD PAINT
- PAINTBRUSH
- CHALK

# chalkboard paint storage pots

I love terracotta plant pots—the older and dustier, the better. When we moved into our new house, the lovely owners left behind a potting shed full of them. It seemed a pity to save them for our few herbs, so I decided to bring some into the house as well and use them as storage jars. Adding chalkboard paint, so that you can write your own "labels," makes them look as if they have a purpose and are not just an overspill from the garden.

Chalkboard paint doesn't have to be black—it now comes in a huge range of colors. I was quite tempted by gray.

I tried brushing the paint on in a few different shapes—hearts, squares, and stars—but invariably came back to a traditional oval shape for the labels. It simply looked much more chic.

1. Paint the shape you want for your "label" on the plant pot. You'll probably need two coats to get even coverage. Let the paint dry thoroughly.

2. Using chalk, write or draw whatever you want as the label for your storage jar. You can wipe the chalkboard paint clean with a damp cloth whenever you want to write something new.

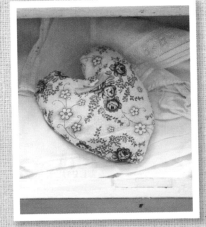

# Chapter 4

# to nest

I've moved house several times in the past few years and as I've accumulated possessions along the way, each place has felt more like a real home than the last. Here in our new house, I'm working my way around each room, adding little personal, quirky touches to give it a cozy, lived-in look.

These projects will show you how you, too, can turn your house into a home with a few special additions.

# hot-water bottle cover

The moment someone says hot water bottle, I think of my Granny. Her hot water bottles always had beautiful homemade covers in the softest velvet, which she'd spent hours embroidering and decorating with antique lace. As long as the bottle is water tight, there is no reason why a cover cannot be exquisite and practical at the same time—and so much prettier than the itchy, gimmicky, store-bought ones.

## INGREDIENTS

- FABRIC
- HOT-WATER BOTTLE
- TAILOR'S CHALK OR FABRIC MARKER PEN
- FABRIC SCISSORS
- BEAUTIFUL BUTTONS OR TRIMS FOR DECORATION (OPTIONAL)
- NEEDLE AND THREAD
- PINS
- SEWING MACHINE

### NO SEWING MACHINE?

If you don't have a sewing machine, place the pieces wrong sides together and blanket stitch by hand.

My versions are slightly more simple and, I guess, more practical. The fabric needs to be quite thick—both to keep the heat in, like a tea cozy, and, most importantly, so that you don't burn yourself. The ones I've had most success with are made from old grain sack or hemp. Using vintage also means that the fabric is much softer, as it's been worn in over the years. I don't use a pattern for these because hot-water bottles vary in size.

1. Fold the fabric in half, right sides together. Place the hot water bottle on top, then draw around it with tailor's chalk or a fabric marker pen. Add a 2-in. (5-cm) border all around. Cut out. You will have one piece for the front of the cover and one for the back.

2. If you want to decorate the cover, do so now, before you sew the sides together.

3. Pin the back and front covers right sides together.

4. Taking a ⅝-in. (1.5-cm) seam allowance, machine stitch around the two sides and the bottom edge.

5. Turn the cover right side out. Put the hot-water bottle into its new cover and then finish off the rest by hand. As you can see, I sewed around the top using a blanket stitch to give it a prettier finish. You might also like to add a pretty ribbon around the neck; just attach the ribbon to the back of the cover with a small stitch, so that you don't lose it.

SUPER SOFT
If you want to use something softer, old cashmere sweaters make gorgeous covers.

# teacup candles

Much as I love them, I've never been able to buy myself a teacup candle in a shop. It's probably because I know how cheap and easy they are to make. They're such a professional-looking present that people cant believe they're homemade—definitely one of the most satisfying things to create.

## INGREDIENTS

- VINTAGE TEACUP
- CANDLE WAX
- OLD CAN
- CANDLE WICK
- SCISSORS
- WICK HOLDER
- WICK CENTERING TOOL (OR TWO PENCILS AND SOME ADHESIVE TAPE)
- NON-STICK SAUCEPAN
- WOODEN SKEWER

I have a real thing for old china and it's doubly pleasing to find a use for it that is decorative and practical. I think the key to creating a beautiful candle is down to the choice of china. My worst nightmare is a brand new, "vintage look" cup: the machine-printed patterns deprive the china of any character.

Vintage china can be seriously expensive, but the joy of it is the pieces don't need to match and small cracks just add to the charm. eBay has thousands of discount stores selling ravishing cups and saucers for next to nothing. Thrift stores are another great place to hunt for beauties. You need patience to wade through the rubbish but the joy, when you find just one perfect vision, will make all the effort worthwhile.

Don't limit yourself to cups and saucers. Sugar bowls, little vases, eggcups, and jugs also make perfect vessels.

You can, of course, add scent and color to your candles. The easiest way to add color is to grate a wax crayon into the wax while it's melting. For scented candles, put a few drops of your favorite essential oil in the melted wax.

If you can't get hold of any new wax, you can always melt down any old candles you have lying around at home. Just make sure that you use tongs to pick out the old wicks, so that you don't burn yourself.

WHICH WAX?
I like to use eco soya wax, as it burns at a lower temperature than paraffin wax and is gentler on the vintage teacups. It also dries more evenly.

1. Start by measuring out the wax. Fill the vintage cup up with wax, one and a half times. Put the wax in the old can.

2. Half fill the saucepan with water, place the old can in it, and place the saucepan on a low heat to melt the wax.

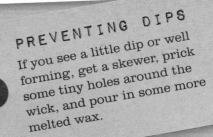

## PREVENTING DIPS

If you see a little dip or well forming, get a skewer, prick some tiny holes around the wick, and pour in some more melted wax.

3. Cut a length of candle wick the height of the cup plus 2 in. (5 cm), and pull it through a wick centering tool. Place the wick centering tool in the bottom of the cup, making sure it is centered.

4. Alternatively, tape the wick between two pencils, making sure it protrudes 1½ in. (4 cm) above the top of the cup. Place the pencils horizontally on the rim of the cup, making sure the bottom of the wick is in the center of the cup. Very carefully pour in the molten wax, until it is just ½ in. (1 cm) below the rim of the cup, and leave to dry. It will take at least half an hour. Try not to move the candles while they are drying.

5. When the wax has set, trim the wick and your teacup candle is complete.

# pillow cover

I started making pillows after I found a divine piece of vintage printed cotton in my favorite French market. Surprisingly for me, it wasn't printed with stripes or roses, but with exuberant parrots. It sat on my desk for a couple of weeks, desperately needing a home. It would have been a pity to cut it up to cover a notebook. I wanted a way to show it off and a pillow cover was the obvious solution.

Zippers are not one of my strong points, so I came up with a simpler fold contraption to close it. I always try to add beautiful trims: mini white pom-poms are one of my favorites and I also adore glass beads trims, although they're not particularly Cub friendly. If I'm using a vintage fabric, I don't mind using a new trim and vice versa. A new fabric can be made to look a bit more loved with some faded, old trimming attached.

Grain sacks and French ticking are my favorite fabrics to use for pillows. Real grain sacks can be expensive, but there are lots of replica ones about that can often be just as gorgeous. If you can't get to a shop or market that sells them, eBay and the online shop Parna are grain-sack heaven.

1. Cut two pieces of fabric for the back of the pillow measuring 21 x 16 in. (53 x 40 cm). Cut a third piece for the front, 21 in. (53 cm) square.

2. Fold over ⅜ in. (1 cm) and then another ⅜ in (1 cm) along one long side of each of the pieces of fabric for the back, pin in place, and machine stitch.

3. Place the fabric for the front right side up on your work surface. Pin or baste (tack) your chosen trim (if using) around the edge of the front, with the trim facing inward. Place the two pieces for the back of the pillow right side down on top, aligning the raw edges and with the hemmed edges overlapping each other.

4. Pin, then machine stitch the pieces together around all four edges, taking a ⅜-in. (1-cm) seam. Turn right side out.

5. Cut the ribbon into six 5-in. (12.5-cm) lengths. Mark three evenly spaced points along the split in the back of the pillow and stitch a pair of ribbons to each point, one on each back piece.

6. Insert the pillow form (cushion pad), tie up the ribbons, and you're done!

## INGREDIENTS

- ¾ YD (70 CM) FABRIC, 44 IN. (112 CM) WIDE
- TAPE MEASURE
- FABRIC SCISSORS
- SEWING MACHINE
- NEEDLE AND THREAD
- APPROX. 82 IN. (208 CM) OF YOUR CHOSEN TRIM (OPTIONAL)
- 30 IN. (75 CM) RIBBON, 1 IN. (2.5 CM) WIDE, TO FASTEN
- 20-IN. (50-CM) SQUARE FEATHER PILLOW FORM (CUSHION PAD)

## NEAT AND TRIM

I feel a pillow doesn't look finished without some kind of a border. Pay a visit to a specialist ribbon shop to find inspiration and more trims and tassels than you'll know what to do with.

# party bunting

If someone says the word "bunting," I immediately think of happy times. Our wonderful friend Sam made miles and miles of it for our wedding, and now every time I see it at other people's parties and weddings it reminds me of our special day.

## INGREDIENTS

- PAPER
- PENCIL AND RULER
- FABRIC
- PINKING SHEARS
- READY-MADE BIAS BINDING, ½ IN. (13 MM) WIDE
- NEEDLE AND THREAD OR SEWING MACHINE

Bunting is mostly associated with big parties and festivals, but I can never understand why it's not used more for everyday decorations. The Cub was given some when he was born and it's been hanging in his bedroom ever since. It looks gorgeous and also faintly educational, as each flag is stitched with a letter of the alphabet.

There's no end to the ways in which you can personalize bunting and it's also a great way to use up remnants of fabric, especially if you like lots of added pattern and color in a room.

1. Draw a triangle on a piece of paper and cut it out to use as a template. My triangles measured 12 in. (30 cm) across the top.

2. Pin the template to your fabric and cut around it, using pinking shears to avoid the edges fraying. Repeat until you have enough flags.

3. Leaving at least 16 in. (40 cm) of binding at each end, space the flags evenly along the bias binding, and pin in place. My flags are spaced 8 in. (20 cm) apart.

4. Machine or hand stitch along the top of the bias binding to secure the flags in place.

DREAM THEME
Carry on a nursery theme by making co-ordinating bunting. Someone loves pirates? Choose a fabric decorated with parrots and pirate ships.

INGREDIENTS

– LAMPSHADE
– ROLL OF RIBBON
– CLEAR-DRYING GLUE
  (I USE LATEX-BASE
  ADHESIVE)
– POM-POM TRIM
– SCISSORS
– GLUE GUN OR CLEAR-
  DRYING SUPERGLUE

# ribbon lampshade

I've never really given much thought to lampshades: they've always been one of those things that are just "there." But the more I go to vintage sales and fairs, the more I am drawn to them. I'm learning that they can actually be a rather quirky addition to a room and are surprisingly simple to create at home. So having overlooked them for years, I'm gradually working my way around the house, jazzing up our safe cream card ones to make them a bit more eye-catching.

1. Cut a long length of the ribbon you are using. Dab a tiny bit of glue on the inside of the lampshade, on the rim.

2. Start wrapping the ribbon around lampshade, overlapping the lengths as you go. The shorter the ribbon the easier it will be, as you're less likely to get tangled, so you'll have to keep joining in new lengths. When you reach the end of each length, glue it down, just as you did at the start. Always try to hide the joins by gluing the next length of ribbon directly on top of the previous one.

3 Measure out the length of pom-pom trim you need and glue it on with a glue gun. If you don't have a glue gun, use a clear-drying superglue instead. Stick it down bit by bit around the bottom of the shade.

# lavender bags

Lavender has always been one of my favorite scents. I suppose its miraculous, sleep-inducing qualities are one reason. The other is how much it reminds me of our old life in France. One of my happiest times of year there was when the fields, almost overnight, turned a deep purple, which was a sign that the flowers were ready. We could harvest our crop and replace the faded lavender bunches with fresh ones.

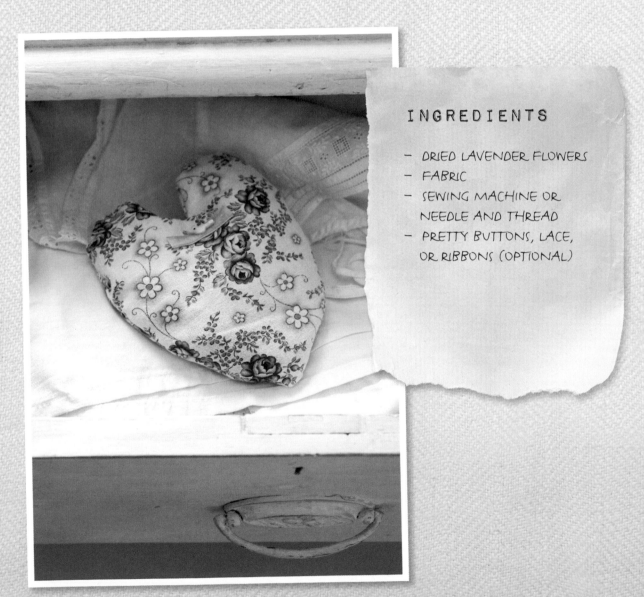

## INGREDIENTS

- DRIED LAVENDER FLOWERS
- FABRIC
- SEWING MACHINE OR NEEDLE AND THREAD
- PRETTY BUTTONS, LACE, OR RIBBONS (OPTIONAL)

They're not really a necessity, but I do seem to have lavender bags all over our house—dotted around in sock drawers, under the bed, in the bed, wherever the Cub's dropped them on his travels. And thinking about it, just having one on my bedside table feels like a security blanket—my ticket to a good night's sleep.

You can make lavender bags in any size, shape, or form you like. The fabric just acts as a house for the lavender, keeping it safely contained inside. When I'm making them for the underwear drawers or somewhere hidden from view, I just make simple square ones—but the ones that live in my bed each night deserve to be prettier, with beautiful touches of ribbons, antique buttons, and lace.

1. Cut out the shape that you want the bag to be: a square, heart, or round shape are obvious ones to use. You will need two of these shapes—one for the front of the bag and one for the back.

2. Place the two shapes right sides together and machine or hand stitch around three sides. (If you're making a heart or a circular shape, sew three-quarters of the way around the bag.)

3. Turn the bag right side out and fill it with lavender. I use a teaspoon to fill the bags, otherwise most of the lavender ends up on the floor.

4. When the bag is about three-quarters full, turn the raw edges under and whipstitch by hand to close the bag.

5. If you wish, hand stitch a pretty button, piece of lace, or ribbon bow to the front of the bag for decoration.

### SMALL STITCHES

Whether you're stitching by hand or by machine, use small stitches to prevent any lavender from escaping through the seams.

# decorative sticks

You might look at this page and wonder what on earth these are. I'm afraid there's no great mystery to them. They don't "do" anything or have any secret purpose. They are purely decorative and sit all over our home, propped up on various sills and mantelpieces. I cannot stop making them. There's something incredibly therapeutic about it. Maybe I should call them "healing sticks" instead.

I went to an antiques market a few months ago and came home with a huge glass bell jar full of vintage spools of cotton thread. They are all beautiful shades of pinks and creams, which meant that getting the gradual color gradient that I wanted for the sticks was something I didn't even need to think about.

The Cub and I went out hunting together in the woods for sticks. There's no rule about the size and thickness of sticks you use, but I feel some kind of uniformity works best. Mine were all about ¾ in. (2 cm) thick and more or less the same length, give or take 2 in. (5 cm) or so.

The thread color you use depends entirely on your taste. Mine are all quite tonal, but my next batch is going to be much brighter, with the odd sparkly metallic thread thrown in here and there.

To make, simply wrap the thread around and around each stick until you have the thickness you want.

**THICK OR THIN?**
The thinner the thread, the smoother it looks. The only downside is that you need a lot more of it. Embroidery floss (thread) also works well.

INGREDIENTS

– AS MANY STICKS AS YOU
  WANT TO DECORATE
– LOTS OF COLORED THREADS

# templates

These templates are for the linen tote bag on pages 114–119.

**Bag base**
Cut one base piece in the main fabric and one base piece in the lining fabric.

This template is shown at 50% of its original size, so enlarge it by 200%.

**Bag handle**
Cut two handles in the main fabric and two handles in the lining fabric.
This template is shown at 50% of its original size, so enlarge it by 200%.

Place on fold of fabric

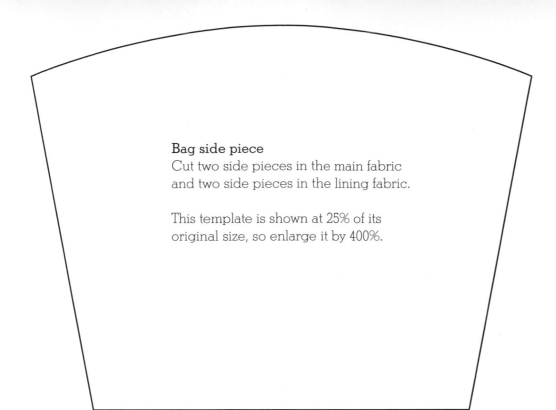

**Bag side piece**
Cut two side pieces in the main fabric
and two side pieces in the lining fabric.

This template is shown at 25% of its
original size, so enlarge it by 400%.

**Pocket**
Cut one pocket in the main fabric and
one pocket in the lining fabric.

This template is shown at the size it is
used, so there is no need to enlarge it.

# index

# acknowledgments

So many people have been involved in creating this book with me. It seems unfair that I should take all the credit. I have been so lucky to be inundated with so many friends and family offering help from start to finish; thank you to each and every one of you.

I would like to say a huge, extra-special thank you:

To my husband, Chaz. For all your love and support. For your endless patience and constant belief. For your ideas and your excellent crafting skills. For calming me when it got too much. I couldn't have done it without you.

To Mama. This book should really have your name on the cover, too. I don't know where to start in thanking you for all your help. Your editing, your ideas, your sensational crafting, your looking after the Cub. For being on call 24/7 to advise and listen. I could go on and on. You are my inspiration. Thank you, Mama. I am more grateful than words can say.

To Da. For all your encouragement and support. For the hours of distracting golf play with the Cub. And for letting us take over your home for days on end.

To Cindy Richards, Gillian Haslam, Sally Powell, and Louise Leffler at CICO Books. I am so grateful to you all for taking a chance on me, giving me this incredible opportunity to create this book. It has been a dream come true and I have loved every second. Thank you for your kindness, patience, and help in turning my visions into a reality.

To Claire Richardson, photographer extraordinaire. For capturing my ideas better than I dreamed was possible. For all your help with the technical bits! For your ideas, styling, and energy from start to finish.

To Clare Hulton. Without you, this book would still be a daydream. Thank you for making me realize that everything is possible!

To Suze, the most patient person on the planet. Thank you for your never-ending help with the Cub, for fuelling us with sensational lunches, and for your continual interest and enthusiasm.

To Samantha Jones, for your genius apron and peg-bag skills, for your help with Wolf and your excitement and enthusiasm toward this book.

To Ned, Tom, and Amanda, for being at the end of a phone whenever I needed you.

To Poppy Delevingne for your encouragement and for being so generous with your time, help, and ideas from start to finish.

To Chloe Delevingne for coming to my rescue.

To Sarah Hoggett for your wonderful editing and for rescuing me from a technology-induced breakdown.

To my baby boys, Wolf and Rafferty, the most divine and special Cubs on the planet.